jacques pépin
fast food my way

Photographs by Ben Fink

 Houghton Mifflin Company
Boston | New York

jacques pépin
fast food my way

For information about permission to reproduce selections from
this book, write to Permissions, Houghton Mifflin Company,
215 Park Avenue South, New York, New York 10003.

Visit our Web site: www.houghtonmifflinbooks.com.

Library of Congress Cataloging-in-Publication Data
    Pépin, Jacques.
      Jacques Pépin fast food my way /
    photographs by Ben Fink.
        p. cm.
    Includes index.
    ISBN 0-618-39312-9
    1. Quick and easy cookery.   I. Title.
    TX833.5.P47 2004
    641.5'55 — dc22   2004047279

Book design by Ralph Fowler
Prop styling by Roy Finamore

The publisher gratefully acknowledges
Villeroy & Boch for supplying the flatware and
many of the dishes used in the photographs.

Printed in China
CAC 10 9 8 7 6 5

*To Gloria,
Claudine,
and Shorey,
my loves*

Contents

Introduction

Yes, I was born and kitchen-trained in France. But even after having spent more than four decades in the United States, people still think of me as a French chef and associate me with French cuisine. They also have the impression that French food or any of my cooking requires long, elaborate preparation. Nothing could be further from the truth.

More often than not, I prefer simple, straightforward food that can be prepared quickly. My wife, Gloria, and I often go out together to do errands or shopping, which usually takes longer than we planned. So we come home hungry. The first thing I do is put a pot of water on to boil. Only then do I take off my jacket and raid the refrigerator for vegetables. By the time I've grated some zucchini, carrots, and onions—and whatever else I might find—the water is boiling. The grated vegetables cook in moments; I add some instant grits and chopped salad greens for body, and presto: we have homemade soup. Dishes like this—you'll find the recipe for Instant Vegetable Soup on page 46—are comforting for a family and elegant enough to serve guests.

This book pays tribute to a very simple cuisine—my "fast food." Some of the recipes are not necessarily quick but none requires much work, and all fit nicely into today's fast-paced lifestyles. Take a look at my Oven-Baked Salmon on page 118. It takes only moments to season (you can do this in the morning, if you've planned ahead), and you put it in a low oven on the same platter you're planning to serve it on. While the fish bakes, you can make the sauce, serve drinks to guests, or just set the table and relax. The fish will be moist and meltingly tender,

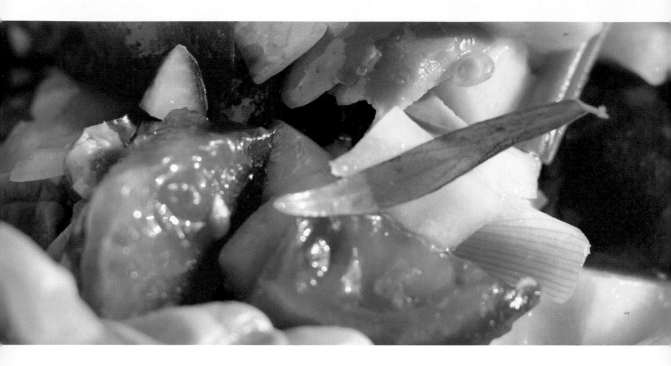

guaranteed to win praise. After the meal, you have only the platter to clean—not a roasting pan.

Although I commend anyone who will take hours preparing a dish from scratch, I'm not a snob about cooking. I know that "homemade" doesn't necessarily translate into superlative food. Most French people would not think of baking their own bread or croissants or making their own pâté, because these items are readily available and of good quality at local markets.

My sister-in-law, for instance, who works in Paris and commutes on the train to the suburbs, stops at the market on her way home and picks up some bread, vegetables, and perhaps a veal roast. When she gets home, she browns the roast in a pressure cooker with an onion, adds some potatoes, puts the lid on the pressure cooker, and then goes upstairs to change. About thirty minutes later, after a leisurely aperitif, dinner is ready.

A schedule like this can be yours, too. Great food—easier than going out for conventional fast food and certainly better for you—takes only minimal planning.

When I don't feel like slaving in the kitchen for hours (and I rarely do) or when guests drop by unexpectedly, I turn unhesitatingly to convenience foods. Cans are a treasure in the pantry, whether they contain anchovies, tomatoes, peaches, tuna, or beans. I can easily transform these ingredients into fast and elegant dishes, as you will see in these pages. Cheese, olives, smoked salmon and trout, and nuts can all be used to great advantage. Good olive oils, vinegars, salsas—even mayonnaise and ketchup—are the base for marinades and sauces to enhance your meals. Store-bought brioche and pound cake become part of quick and delicious desserts, as do shortbread cookies.

Proper techniques and good equipment make your kitchen life easier. Sharp knives, sturdy vegetable peelers, thick, heavy pots (some nonstick), good solid cookie sheets, and rubber spatulas are all essential. While I don't rely on gadgets, I make use of my blender and food processor regularly, as well as my pressure cooker. I also rely on my microwave oven, which is ideal for reheating anything sticky that would leave a messy pan and is the key to making a quick baked potato. While the oven is heating, we pop the potatoes in the microwave. They're nearly done by the time the oven is hot, and we finish them in the oven, so they get the crisp skin we love.

My fast food is best shared with friends, along with a bottle of wine. Cook some of these dishes together; you'll be surprised at how quickly the food comes to the table, and you'll enjoy the camaraderie. After following my recipes a few times, you'll start to develop a "fast-food" style of your own.

You will see that most of the dishes in this book are designed to serve four. You have more people at your table? All these recipes double easily. When you're putting together a meal in a hurry, take a few extra seconds to make it look special. Fresh herbs add a beautiful accent and bright flavor to dishes, and I use them lavishly, since they are so plentiful in my garden. But don't hesitate to change the garnishes I suggest. Trust your instincts and your sense of taste. They will lead you. Eventually, you'll transform my simple dishes into your own personal cuisine.

Happy cooking and happy times!

Menus

as seen on public television

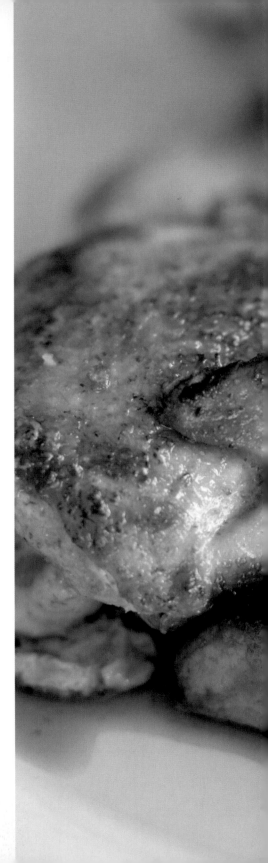

Crab Cakes in Red Sauce (page 133)
Pasta, Ham, and Vegetable Gratin (page 112)
Romaine and Radicchio with Salsa Dressing (page 68)
Big Almond Macaroons with Apricot Filling (page 178)

❧

Summertime Pasta (page 110)
Red Snapper with Tomatoes and Cream (page 127)
Asparagus with Shallots (page 90)
Two Raspberry Gratins (page 202)

❧

Chopped Chicken Livers with Spinach Salad (page 37)
Glazed Salmon in Mirin (page 120)
Silky Chestnut and Apple Puree (page 93)
Warm Chocolate Cakes with Apricot-Cognac Sauce (page 198)

❧

Silky Tomato Soup with Spinach Coulis (page 48)
Little Shrimp Casseroles (page 137)
Toasted Bread and Mozzarella (page 39)
Rhubarb and Berry Crumble (page 184)

❧

Tomato Tartare with Tomato Water Sauce (page 80)
Rigatoni and Mussels with Saffron (page 140)
Creamy Lima Bean Gratin (page 98)
Strawberry Panachée (page 204)

⬿

Sea Bass Gravlax with Cucumber (page 26)
Chicken Tonnato (page 148)
Summer Salad (page 67)
Chestnut and Chocolate Cake (page 193)

⬿

Corn and Hominy Chowder (page 53)
Red Snapper with Mussels and Chorizo (page 124)
Puree of Peas with Mint and Cilantro (page 99)
Banana Bourbon Coupe (page 189)

⬿

Instant Vegetable Soup (page 46)
Halibut on Fresh Polenta with Pepper Oil (page 116)
Broad Beans with Shallots (page 88)
Hasty Pudding with Apricot Sauce (page 197)

⬿

Asparagus Custards (page 85)
Slow-Cooked Tuna Steaks with Tomato Relish (page 123)
Sautéed Plantains (page 100)
Apple Skillet Cake (page 179)

⬿

Bow-Tie Pasta with Fried Eggs and Cheese (page 62)
Shrimp and Scallop Pillows on Boston Lettuce (page 129)
Crusty Tomato Savory (page 101)
Grapefruit Gratinée (page 192)

⬿

Codfish Brandade (page 20)
Chicken Breasts with Garlic and Parsley (page 148)
Broccoli Rabe and Pea Fricassee (page 86)
Chocolate Hazelnut Brownie Cake (page 194)

⬿

Scrambled Eggs with Mushrooms and Truffles (page 58)
Sautéed Quail with Raita (page 152)
Cubed Potatoes with Garlic and Sage (page 109)
Pears in Honeyed Wine (page 207)

❧

Scrambled Eggs on Tomato *Jus* (page 59)
Grilled Striped Bass with Pimiento Relish (page 117)
Cauliflower with Scallions and Sesame Oil (page 89)
Pink Grapefruit Terrine (page 190)

❧

For a Buffet
Asparagus with Croutons and Chorizo (page 84)
Melon and Prosciutto (page 43)
Oven-Baked Salmon with Sun-Dried Tomato and
    Salsa Mayonnaise (page 118)
Sweet Cheese Medley (page 40)
Almond Cake with Berries (page 176)

❧

Soupy Rice with Peas (page 106)
Fast Lobster Fricassee (page 134)
Broccoli Puree with Brown Butter (page 91)
Vanilla Praline Dessert (page 217)

❧

Egg and Tomato Gratin (page 60)
Stuffed Scallops on Mushroom Rice (page 138)
Greens with Quick Cream Dressing (page 73)
Pineapple Wedges in Caramel (page 213)

❧

Smoked Trout Salad with Horseradish Cream (page 28)
Chicken on Mashed Cauliflower with Red Hot Salsa
    (page 146)
Mock Tiramisù (page 215)

Scallop Seviche and Guacamole (page 32)
Beef Short Rib, Mushroom, and Potato Stew (page 158)
Champagne on Fruit "Rocks" (page 219)

Smoked Salmon Timbales (page 25)
Thirty-Minute Cassoulet (page 167)
Zucchini and Tomato Salad (page 70)
Oranges and Cream Cheese (page 206)

Tomato and Mozzarella Fans (page 78)
Veal Roast (page 160)
Skillet Endives (page 96)
Pear Brown Betty (page 214)

Salmon Tartare on Cauliflower Salad (page 24)
Breaded Pork Scaloppine with Mushroom Sauce (page 163)
Chickpea Ragout (page 95)
Caramelized Peaches (page 208)

Lobster Salad with Tarragon (page 31)
Pressure-Cooker Lamb and White Bean Stew (page 170)
Asian Eggplant Salad (page 77)
Pinot Noir Granité (page 199)

Bean Puree with Anchovies or Smoked Oysters (page 34)
Wonton Cannelloni in Tomato Sauce (page 111)
Parsley and Pumpkin Seed Salad (page 72)
Caramelized Apple–Granola Timbales (page 181)

Devil Shrimp (page 36)
Sausage and Potato Packet (page 168)
Mushroom and Walnut Salad in Sour Cream Dressing
   (page 74)
Apple Peel Granité with Apple Puree (page 185)

Salmon Rolls on Fennel Salad (page 22)
Broiled Lamb Chops with Spinach (page 169)
Baked Potatoes with Chive Sour Cream (page 108)
Crepes with Banana-Rum Filling (page 187)

Mushroom Velouté with Almonds (page 50)
Instant Beef Tenderloin Stew (page 156)
Mushroom and Raisin Chutney (page 102)
Apple, Pecan, and Apricot Crumble (page 182)

More ideas for quick dishes

Quesadillas. I love quesadillas and often make them as an hors d'oeuvre. I sprinkle some grated American, manchego, or Monterey Jack cheese on a couple of flour tortillas, add some cilantro and hot salsa or Tabasco to taste, and fold the tortillas in half. Then I cook them in a dash of canola oil in a nonstick pan for a couple of minutes on each side, let them rest for a few minutes, cut them into wedges, and serve.

Cheese crostini. I serve cheese crostini often as an hors d'oeuvre or salad accompaniment. To make them, I arrange leftover slices of baguette on an oiled cookie sheet and top with plum tomato slices, Gruyère, a dash of salt, and plenty of black pepper. I bake them in a hot oven for 6 to 8 minutes, until nicely browned, sprinkle them with a little chopped cilantro or parsley, and serve.

Basil, cheese, fig, and nut bites. A plate of basil, nut meats, figs, and cheese makes a good light lunch or cheese course at a fancy dinner party. I place a few roasted nuts—pecans, walnuts, or almonds—in the center of each of several large basil leaves and serve two per plate, with a slice of ripe Camembert or Brie and a dried fig cut in half.

Baby mozzarella salad. As a first course, a baby mozzarella salad is great. Make use of the bounty of your supermarket deli counter: small mozzarella balls (*bocconcini*), diced red pimientos, pitted black and green olives, sun-dried tomato halves, and capers, if available. Mix these ingredients with a little extra-virgin olive oil, cracked pepper, and a dash of vinegar and serve cupped in a leaf of radicchio on individual plates.

Prosciutto and figs. I like prosciutto sliced very thin. Cut one fresh fig in half and wrap one or two slices of prosciutto around each half, so the flesh of the fig is exposed. Sprinkle black pepper on top and serve with a fresh baguette and a dollop of mascarpone for a treat as good as you will ever get in Italy.

Pico de gallo (the rooster's beak). A standard at any Mexican restaurant, this spicy accompaniment is made with diced tomato, coarsely chopped onion, chopped jalapeño pepper (the amount determined by your tolerance), a lot of cilantro, a little ground cumin, and a dash of ketchup, which I like to add for texture and taste. This is always a hit when served as a dip with tortilla chips.

Avocado halves in red sauce. Avocados are a great favorite of mine, and for a quick first course I often cut them in half, remove the pits with a knife, and, using a large spoon, scoop out the contents from each half. Place an avocado half on each plate and sprinkle with a little coarse salt or *fleur de sel*. In a small bowl, mix together a little mayonnaise with ketchup, Tabasco to taste, and a little water until creamy. Spoon on top of or around the avocado halves and sprinkle with some crushed spicy tortilla chips.

Smoked salmon plate. Smoked salmon (Scottish or Irish is best) is available in most markets. For an elegant first course, arrange two or three slices (depending on size) of good smoked salmon on individual plates. Sprinkle some chopped red onion or scallions, a few capers, and, if you like, some diced cucumber on top. Finish with a few dashes of extra-virgin olive oil and serve with a lemon wedge, a few sprigs of dill or fennel, and buttered black bread.

Smoked whitefish tartine. Gloria loves smoked fish, and I often make this dish for her as a first course. I cover a large piece of pumpernickel or multigrain bread with whipped cream cheese, place pieces of smoked whitefish or trout on top, and sprinkle on some cracked pepper and a few pitted black olives. I serve this open-faced sandwich on top of a bed of watercress or baby spinach with a dash of olive oil on top.

Sardine rolls. Occasionally I make sardine rolls as a first course. I moisten rice paper rounds (available in many markets) to soften them and place two or three canned sardines on each paper, along with some chopped red onion, a strip of pimiento, ground black pepper, and a dash of red wine vinegar. I then roll the papers up tightly and serve two rolls per person on a bed of mesclun salad.

Tuna tomatoes. In summer, when good tomatoes are available, mix a drained can of tuna (preferably packed in oil) with some minced scallions, pitted Kalamata olives, diced anchovy fillets, chopped parsley, and cracked pepper. Cut off the tops of ripe tomatoes and hollow them out with a spoon, reserving and lightly crushing the tomato pulp with a fork and mixing it with a little olive oil, salt, and pepper to create a sauce. Fill the hollow tomatoes with the tuna mixture and serve with some of the sauce for a first course.

Ham cornucopias. For a first course, roll up individual slices of ham into a cornet or cornucopia shape and place each in a flat-bottomed rocks glass or on a plate on top of baby spinach or watercress. Mix diced feta cheese, pitted black olives, and marinated mushrooms—all from your supermarket deli—with a dash of olive oil, cracked pepper, and salt. Spoon into the ham cornucopias and serve.

Cannellini and chorizo soup. I always have the ingredients for this fast, satisfying soup in my pantry and refrigerator. Puree a can of cannellini beans in a blender with enough chicken stock to make a creamy soup. Transfer to a saucepan, add diced chorizo sausage, bring to a boil, sprinkle with salt and pepper to taste, and finish with a little heavy cream. Garnish with chopped chives and croutons.

Cold black bean soup. When friends drop by in the summer, I like to make cold soup. One combination that I love is made in a food processor. Puree a can of black bean soup with a little olive oil, Tabasco, a couple of tablespoons of chopped onion, a crushed clove of garlic, salt, and enough chicken stock to make the mixture creamy. Serve in soup plates, topping each serving with a ribbon of sour cream diluted with a bit of water. Garnish with a few slices of banana and a couple of cilantro leaves.

Peasant soup. For this soup like one my mother used to make, prepare croutons by baking slices of leftover bread in a conventional oven or toaster oven until brown and crisp. Divide the toasted bread among soup bowls, breaking the slices into pieces if they are too large, and grate a generous amount of Gruyère or Jarlsberg on top. Bring a good homemade chicken stock or canned broth to a boil and pour over the croutons and cheese in the bowls. Sprinkle with cracked pepper and a few chopped chives and serve.

Sweet potato chowder. For this easy, delicious soup, pulse cooked fresh or canned plain sweet potatoes (*not* in sweet syrup) in a food processor with chicken stock and salt and pepper to taste until the consistency is to your liking. Add some heavy cream and bring the soup to a boil in a saucepan. Spoon into bowls and top each serving with oven-roasted pumpkin seeds and a sprig of dill.

Lavash pizza. You can make homemade pizza in no time at all using flour tortillas, pita bread, or—my favorite—lavash. After oiling a cookie sheet, I press one of these large flatbread rectangles on the sheet, then turn it over, so it is lightly oiled on both sides. Cover it with sliced tomatoes, some grated mozzarella and Parmesan, cracked pepper, anchovies (optional), and a few dashes of olive oil. Bake in a 425-degree oven for 8 to 10 minutes, then sprinkle with lots of basil leaves torn into coarse pieces.

Shrimp burgers. I discovered these at Dr. Taco while vacationing at Playa del Carmen in Mexico. Put a couple of slices of manchego or mozzarella in a nonstick skillet and place over moderate heat. As the cheese begins to melt, add a few small raw shrimp or pieces of shrimp, salt, some hot salsa or cracked

pepper, and some chopped scallions or chives. Cover and cook over medium heat for a couple of minutes, then slide the cheese-shrimp burger onto half a toasted bun topped with a lettuce leaf and tomato slices.

Red beets in sour cream. For a winter salad, drain a can of sliced red beets and combine the slices with sour cream, cracked pepper, salt, and a dash of red wine vinegar. Serve over endive leaves, with a sprinkling of flat-leaf parsley, tarragon, or basil leaves on top.

Summer salad santé. I make this salad from ingredients directly out of my garden. I pick a bunch each of basil, flat-leaf parsley, and arugula and collect a handful of tarragon leaves and some chives, which I break into pieces. I mix these in a large salad bowl with a little lemon juice, extra-virgin olive oil, and salt and pepper to taste. It's excellent with good country bread.

Apricot sherbet. For a quick dessert, puree a can of apricot halves in heavy syrup in a blender for about 30 seconds to infuse the mixture with air. Transfer the puree to a glass baking dish so

it forms a fairly thin layer that will cool quickly, and place it in the freezer until semisoft. (If making the sherbet ahead, freeze the puree until solid, and then, several hours before serving, soften it in the refrigerator until you can scoop it out of the dish. For a creamier result, process for a few seconds in a food processor.) Spoon into chilled glasses, top with pistachio nuts, and serve each dessert with a cookie.

Blueberries in raspberry sauce with ice cream. Any berries are great for a summertime dessert. Mix some blueberries in a bowl with raspberry jam and a little cognac or water. Spoon into cocktail glasses, top each with a small scoop of vanilla ice cream, and serve with a cookie.

Guava delicioso. My wife loves guava, so I serve a simple dessert of little chunks of canned guava paste on Ritz crackers with a dollop of cream cheese on top. To finish, I push a basil leaf into the cream cheese and sprinkle it with a few pistachio nuts.

Pineapple slices in kirsch with sherbet. A pineapple slice flavored with kirschwasser (cherry brandy) is a classic combination from my years in the great kitchens of Paris. Arrange a fresh or canned pineapple slice with some of the syrup or a sprinkling of sugar on each dessert plate and pour a little kirsch on top. Place a small scoop of fruit sherbet (lemon, orange, tangerine, strawberry, or raspberry) in the hollow center of each slice. Garnish with mint leaves and serve with a cookie.

Ricotta honey mix. For a fast and easy dessert, place a graham cracker on each plate and put a large spoonful of ricotta on top. Pour a couple tablespoons of honey over and around the ricotta and sprinkle on some diced dried apricots and dark raisins. This dessert is better still with the addition of a few drops of Grand Marnier.

Pineapple frosties. Ideal for hot summer nights at the beach, these tasty cold drinks are a cinch to make. Emulsify a mixture of canned crushed pineapple in syrup, crushed ice, a little lime juice, and dark rum in a food processor. Spoon into glasses, garnish with mint sprigs, and serve.

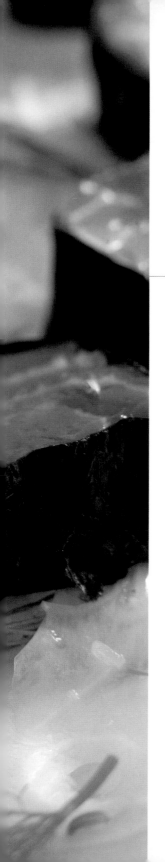

Appetizers and first courses

Codfish brandade

This elegant puree of salted codfish serves four, but it makes sense to double the quantity and freeze the remainder in small gratin dishes, about 1¼ cups per dish. This way, you'll have some on hand ready to be baked and served on toast when guests, expected or not, arrive.

Be sure to taste the finished brandade to see if it needs salt, as the desalting procedure can make it bland. ❧ *4 servings*

Put the desalted cod in a saucepan, cover with cold water, and bring to a boil. Reduce the heat to low and boil gently for 5 minutes. Drain in a colander. When the fish is cool enough to handle, remove the skin, if any, and reserve, and remove and discard the bones and sinew from the cod. Break the fish into 1-inch pieces and return the pieces to the saucepan with the skin, potatoes, milk, garlic, and fennel seeds. Bring to a boil, reduce the heat to low and boil gently, uncovered, for 20 to 25 minutes, until the potatoes and the fish are tender.

Transfer the contents of the pan to a food processor and process for about 10 seconds. Add the pepper and continue processing while you pour in the oil through the feeding tube. The mixture should be smooth. Taste, add salt if needed, and process just until the salt is incorporated. (You'll have about 2½ cups.)

Serve warm on toasted baguette slices.

About 12 ounces salted codfish, soaked for 6–8 hours in cold water to remove excess salt, with the water changed twice at even intervals during the soaking process

1¼ cups cubed (1-inch) peeled potatoes

1 cup milk

6 small or 4 large garlic cloves, peeled and crushed

¼ teaspoon fennel seeds

¼ teaspoon freshly ground black pepper

¼ cup extra-virgin olive oil

Salt, if needed

About 16 slices (each ½ inch thick) from a baguette, browned on a cookie sheet in a 400-degree oven for 6–8 minutes

Variations

To serve the brandade as a gratin: Spoon the brandade into a 4-cup gratin dish or shallow baking dish, and set aside or freeze to finish later. When ready to bake, heat the oven to 425 degrees. Sprinkle 1 tablespoon grated Parmesan cheese on top of the brandade and bake for about 20 minutes (at least 10 minutes longer if the gratin is frozen), or until it is nicely browned on top. Serve with the toasted baguette slices.

To serve the brandade as a gratin with 5-minute eggs: Lower 4 eggs into boiling water to cover and cook at a gentle boil for 5 minutes. Cool under cold water, peel, and leave in the cold water until you are ready to finish the gratin. Meanwhile, prepare the gratin as directed above and heat the oven to 425 degrees. Bake the gratin for 15 minutes, then remove it and make 4 evenly spaced depressions in the crusted top. Place a cold egg in each depression. Pour ⅓ cup heavy cream on top of the eggs and the gratin, then sprinkle the eggs with ½ tablespoon grated Parmesan cheese. Return the gratin to the oven for 5 minutes longer, or until browned on top. Serve immediately with the toasted baguette slices.

About salt cod

Salt cod, or bacalao, is available in most supermarkets and fish stores. I prefer the cod from Norway.

Salt cod must be desalted in cold water as the first step in its preparation. Soak it overnight or for as long as a day, changing the water at least twice. Keep it in the refrigerator, covered, while it soaks. Sometimes salt cod comes with bones, which should be removed after you cook it. If the cod comes with skin, I blend it into the brandade, as it lends a creamy texture.

Salmon rolls on fennel salad

This recipe is particularly useful for a party, since the rolls are easy to make, flavorful, and attractive. The salmon medallions cure for about an hour in the salt, sugar, and pepper mixture.

The fennel salad is good by itself or as a garnish for grilled fish or meat. Nori, the toasted seaweed used for sushi, is available in many Asian markets and specialty stores.

≈ 12 servings

For the salmon rolls: Cut the trimmed salmon fillet into 3 lengthwise strips. Since the strip near the belly is thinner, fold it on itself so that each strip is about 1½ inches thick and 7 to 8 inches long.

Rinse the nori sheets briefly under cool running water, wetting them on both sides. Arrange them flat in one layer on the table, and place a salmon strip in the center of each of 3 sheets to make 3 rolls. Bring the sides of the nori sheets up to enclose the salmon strips, sealing by pressing the edges together where they meet, then wrap each salmon roll in another nori sheet to make a thicker, stronger covering.

Combine the salt, pepper, and sugar in a small bowl. Line a cookie sheet with plastic wrap and sprinkle half the salt mixture on top. On a cutting board, cut each salmon roll crosswise into ½-inch-thick slices. (You should have about 36 slices, 12 from each roll.) Arrange the slices, cut sides down, on the cookie sheet. Sprinkle the remaining salt mixture on top of the slices, cover them with plastic wrap, and refrigerate for at least 1 hour before serving.

Salmon rolls

- 2 pounds center-cut salmon fillet (about 1¾ pounds with skin and any fatty black surface flesh removed)
- 6 sheets nori (each about 8 inches square)
- 1 tablespoon kosher salt
- 1 teaspoon freshly ground black pepper
- 1 teaspoon sugar

Fennel salad

- 2 small fennel bulbs (about 1½ pounds total), trimmed of tough outside leaves or ribs (trimmed weight about 1 pound)
- 3 tablespoons good olive oil
- 2 teaspoons grated lemon zest
- 2 tablespoons fresh lemon juice
- ¼ teaspoon salt
- ¼ teaspoon Tabasco sauce
- 2 teaspoons fennel seeds
  Extra-virgin olive oil (optional)

For the fennel salad: Shave the fennel bulb into paper-thin slices on a Japanese slicer or mandoline (you will have about 5 cups). Combine the olive oil, lemon zest and juice, salt, Tabasco, and fennel seeds in a medium bowl. Add the fennel, and toss to coat it with the dressing. Arrange some fennel on each plate and top with a few slices of the salmon rolls. If desired, drizzle with the olive oil.

❮❮ MAKE AHEAD
The salmon rolls can be prepared 1 to 2 days in advance.

Salmon tartare on cauliflower salad

Cauliflower salad makes a terrific accompaniment to salmon. For a fancy presentation, arrange the salad inside a 4-inch ring on each plate. (These rings are available in metal or plastic, or you can make your own with a piece of plastic pipe or a small tuna fish can with the lid and bottom removed.) If you prefer, simply spoon a layer of cauliflower onto each plate and cover it with a layer of tartare.

It is important to cut the salmon coarsely by hand rather than chop it in a food processor, which tends to make it gummy or pasty.

4 servings

For the salmon tartare: No more than 30 minutes before serving, combine all the ingredients in a bowl and refrigerate.

For the cauliflower salad: Bring ¾ cup water to a boil in a skillet. Add the cauliflower florets, bring the water back to a boil, cover, and boil over high heat for 4 to 5 minutes, until tender. Drain off any remaining water, chop the cauliflower coarsely, and combine it in a bowl with the remaining ingredients.

For the garnish: Using an egg slicer, cut each egg into vertical slices, then pivot the slices together 90 degrees in the slicer and cut them horizontally to create coarse egg strips. (Alternatively, you can slice the egg with a sharp knife.) Mix the eggs with the basil in a small bowl, then divide the mixture among four plates, arranging it in a ring around the edge of each plate.

Place a metal pastry ring about 4 inches across and 2 inches high inside the egg border on each plate and arrange a layer of cauliflower inside each ring. Cover with a layer of salmon tartare. Carefully remove the rings. (Alternatively, spoon the cauliflower mixture inside the egg border on each plate and cover with the tartare.) Serve immediately.

Salmon tartare

- 12 ounces salmon flesh with skin and any fatty black surface tissue removed, cut into ½-inch pieces (about 1½ cups)
- 2½ tablespoons chopped red onion
- 1 tablespoon chopped fresh chives
- 1 tablespoon drained capers
- 2 teaspoons good olive oil
- 1 teaspoon rice wine vinegar
- ½ teaspoon salt
- ¼ teaspoon freshly ground black pepper

Cauliflower salad

- 10 ounces cauliflower florets
- 1 tablespoon good olive oil
- 1 tablespoon chopped red onion
- 1 tablespoon Dijon-style mustard
- 1 teaspoon red wine vinegar
- ½ teaspoon salt
- ¼ teaspoon freshly ground pepper

Garnish

- 2 hard-cooked large eggs, peeled
- 2 tablespoons shredded fresh basil

Smoked salmon timbales

This is one of those easy dishes that I make with ingredients that are usually near at hand. The timbales are particularly beautiful, despite taking only a few minutes to put together.

I cut the onion and apple very thin with a mandoline or Japanese slicer.

≈ 4 servings

Using four glass dishes with a ¾-cup capacity, such as custard cups, layer the ingredients into each dish as follows: divide the chives among the bowls, then spoon 1 tablespoon of the goat cheese into each bowl. Press half a slice of the salmon on top and add 1 slice of the onion and 1 slice of the apple. Sprinkle a little of the black pepper over the apple, then press the other half of the salmon slice on top. Add another tablespoon of the goat cheese to each dish, then a slice of the onion and a slice of the apple. Finish each timbale with a dash of black pepper on top. Cover the dishes with plastic wrap and refrigerate until serving time.

For the garnish: Mix the capers, cucumber, salt, and olive oil in a bowl. At serving time, unmold each timbale onto a plate, and sprinkle the garnish around the timbales. Serve with toast or baguette slices.

2 tablespoons minced
  fresh chives

4 ounces soft goat cheese
  (about 8 tablespoons)

4 large slices smoked salmon
  (about 6 ounces total),
  cut in half

8 very thin slices red onion

8 thin slices peeled apple

  About 1 teaspoon freshly
  ground black pepper

Garnish

2 tablespoons drained capers

⅓ cup diced (¼-inch) peeled
  cucumber

¼ teaspoon salt

1½ tablespoons good olive oil

  Toast or baguette slices,
  for serving

◄← MAKE AHEAD
  The timbales can be
  prepared a few hours
  ahead and garnished at
  the last moment.

Sea bass gravlax with cucumber

The seasonings in this sea bass gravlax—I use onion, cilantro, and hot pepper—can be varied according to your tastes and what you have on hand. Likewise, if sea bass is not available where you live, substitute the freshest possible fish—freshness is foremost—striped bass, salmon, or red snapper. I incorporate diced crunchy cucumber into the mixture and garnish it with strips of cucumber and a shower of diced tomato, fresh chives, and oil, preferably truffle oil. I like to mold the gravlax into a cylinder using an empty can.

This recipe is easily doubled if you want to serve it as a main course.   *4 servings*

For the sea bass gravlax: Cut the sea bass into ½-inch pieces and mix them in a medium bowl with the onion, cilantro, chile pepper, olive oil, salt, and pepper. Using a vegetable peeler, peel off about 24 long thin strips from the flesh of the unpeeled cucumber (so the strips are edged with peel), and reserve for garnish. Cut enough of the remaining cucumber into ¼-inch pieces to measure about ⅓ cup. Stir the cucumber pieces into the sea bass mixture.

For the tomato garnish: In another bowl, mix together the tomato, chives, mirin, salt, and pepper.

At serving time, place a clean, empty can 2 to 3 inches in diameter with both ends removed in the center of an individual plate and pack one quarter of the sea bass mixture into it. Carefully lift off the mold and repeat this procedure on the three remaining plates. Arrange about 6 of the cucumber strips on each plate, around the molded sea bass. Divide the tomato garnish among the plates, spooning it around the gravlax. If using truffle oil, mix it with the peanut oil, then drizzle the oil(s) on the garnish. Serve immediately.

About mirin

Mirin, a Japanese rice wine with a slightly sweet flavor, can be found in many supermarkets, Asian stores, and specialty shops.

Sea bass gravlax

About 12 ounces sea bass fillet, bones, skin, and sinews removed

2 tablespoons chopped (¼-inch) sweet onion, such as Vidalia

2 tablespoons chopped fresh cilantro

1 teaspoon minced serrano or jalapeño pepper (or more, depending on your tolerance for hot seasonings)

1½ tablespoons extra-virgin olive oil

½ teaspoon salt

¼ teaspoon freshly ground black pepper

1 cucumber

Tomato garnish

1 cup diced (½-inch) peeled and seeded tomato

2 tablespoons minced fresh chives

1 tablespoon mirin or rice wine vinegar

¼ teaspoon salt

¼ teaspoon freshly ground black pepper

1 tablespoon truffle oil (optional)

1 tablespoon peanut oil, plus 1 tablespoon if not using truffle oil

Smoked trout salad with horseradish cream

I learned how to smoke trout when Gloria and I first got married; she was an avid fisherwoman and caught some trout almost every weekend in the Catskills. Commercially smoked trout is usually available in supermarkets, but if you can't find any, substitute smoked whitefish or smoked bluefish.   ❧ *4 servings*

For the trout salad: Remove the skin from the trout; it should slide off easily. Bone the trout by pulling the meat carefully off the bones so that all the small bones stay attached to the long, large central ones. Set aside.

Using an egg slicer, cut the egg into vertical slices, then pivot the slices together 90 degrees in the slicer and cut them horizontally to create thin egg strips. (Alternatively, you can slice the egg with a sharp knife.) Put the egg, tomato, olives, onion, cilantro, salt, pepper, and oil in a bowl and toss together gently.

For the horseradish cream: Mix the ingredients together in a small bowl.

Divide the tomato mixture among four plates. Make a well in the center of each mound. Spoon the sauce into the well in the center of each salad, dividing it evenly. Arrange pieces of trout on top of the sauce, using about half a trout per person. Serve with French bread.

Smoked trout salad

- 2 smoked trout (home-smoked or store-bought); each about 8 ounces with head on)
- 1 large hard-cooked egg, peeled
- 1 cup diced (½-inch) seeded tomato
- 1 cup pitted mixed olives (Kalamata, black, and green), cut into ½-inch pieces
- ⅓ cup finely chopped onion (preferably from a sweet onion, such as Vidalia)
- 5 tablespoons loosely packed fresh cilantro leaves
- ½ teaspoon salt
- ½ teaspoon freshly ground black pepper
- 2 tablespoons good olive oil

Horseradish cream

- ⅓ cup whipped cream cheese
- 1 tablespoon bottled horseradish
- ¼ teaspoon freshly ground black pepper

  Crunchy French bread, for serving

Lobster salad with tarragon

This fresh, flavorful lobster salad couldn't be easier to make or more elegant. Barely cooked lobster flesh is combined with a dressing similar to crème fraîche. The salad is served mounded in Boston lettuce leaves, which add an appealing crunch. You can use the cooking liquid, lobster juices, and bodies to make a tasty Lobster Bisque (page 54).

4 servings

2 live lobsters (each about 1½ pounds)

3 cups water

¼ cup heavy cream

¼ cup sour cream

¼ teaspoon salt

¼ teaspoon freshly ground black pepper

1 teaspoon fresh lemon juice

2 teaspoons finely chopped fresh tarragon, plus a few fresh tarragon leaves, for garnish

1 head Boston lettuce, leaves separated, washed, and dried

Put the lobsters and the water in a large pot, preferably stainless steel, and cover tightly. Bring the water to a boil over high heat, then reduce the heat and boil the lobsters very gently, covered, for 5 minutes. Set the pan aside off the heat, still covered, and cool the lobsters in the cooking liquid for 30 minutes.

Remove the lobsters from the broth; reserve the broth. Break off the lobster claws and tails and remove the meat, reserving any juice that comes out and adding it to the broth. (You should have about 12 ounces meat, about 3 cups broth, and the shells.) Set the meat aside. Discard the shells from the claws and tails and keep the bodies. Lift the shells from the bodies and discard. Break each body, with the small legs attached, into 2 or 3 pieces. Put these pieces in a container with the lobster broth and refrigerate (or freeze) for later use in making the Lobster Bisque.

Whip the heavy cream in a medium bowl for about 30 seconds, just until soft peaks form, then stir in the sour cream, salt, pepper, lemon juice, and chopped tarragon. Add to the reserved lobster meat and toss gently to coat the lobster with the dressing.

Arrange a few of the lettuce leaves in each of four shallow glasses or glass bowls, so that they form a nest. Spoon the lobster salad into the center, decorate with a few tarragon leaves, and serve.

Scallop seviche and guacamole

Super-fresh scallops are best for this dish. The very large ones, the so-called diver scallops, are ideal, but if they are unavailable, buy an equivalent amount of the largest scallops you can find and serve more slices per person. I cure the scallops in a coarse salt; any gray salt, *fleur de sel,* or kosher salt will work well.

I love guacamole and often serve it with aperitifs to friends. (Double this recipe and serve it on its own with spicy tortilla chips, if you like.) The combination of scallops and guacamole is very delicate, but sprinkling spicy chips on top gives the dish texture and an appealingly piquant taste.

≈ *4 servings*

About guacamole

Some people embed an avocado pit in their guacamole to prevent the mixture from darkening. The best method I've found is to press a piece of plastic wrap on top, so it adheres to the guacamole. The avocados must be ripe; if you buy hard, unripe ones, keep them at room temperature for a few days until they are soft to the touch before using.

For the seviche: Cut each of the scallops crosswise into 6 slices, each ½ inch thick. You should have about 24 slices. Sprinkle about ½ teaspoon salt and ¼ teaspoon pepper in the bottom of a shallow baking dish or on a platter, and arrange the slices of scallop on top in a single layer. Sprinkle with the remaining salt and pepper. Press plastic wrap directly on the surface of the scallops and refrigerate for at least 1 hour, or as long as overnight.

For the guacamole: Cut around each avocado, penetrating the skin and flesh, then twist to separate the avocados into halves. Remove the pit from each, and using a spoon, scoop the flesh into a glass bowl large enough to easily hold the remaining ingredients. Crush coarsely with a fork. (You should have about 1¼ cups.)

Add the remaining ingredients. Mix well. Cover tightly with plastic wrap, applying it directly to the surface of the guacamole. Refrigerate if not serving immediately.

At serving time, arrange 6 scallop slices around the circumference of each of four dinner plates, and spoon about ½ cup guacamole in the center. Drizzle the scallops on each plate with about 2 teaspoons olive oil and crumble a few tortilla chips on top of the guacamole. Serve immediately.

◄← MAKE AHEAD
You can cure the scallops the night before serving.

Scallop seviche

- 4 very large sea scallops (diver scallops; 7–8 ounces total)
- 1 teaspoon kosher salt
- ½ teaspoon freshly ground black pepper

Guacamole

- 2 ripe avocados (about 1 pound)
- ½ cup diced (½-inch) tomato, including seeds and juice
- ¼ cup finely chopped onion, put in a sieve and rinsed under cold running water
- 1½ teaspoons finely chopped garlic
- 2 tablespoons minced poblano pepper (or another chile pepper of your choice)
- 3 tablespoons minced scallion
- ¼ cup coarsely chopped fresh cilantro
- 1 tablespoon fresh lemon juice
- 1½ tablespoons extra-virgin olive oil
- ¾ teaspoon kosher salt
- ½ teaspoon Tabasco Green Pepper sauce (or more, if you like)

For serving

About 3 tablespoons extra-virgin olive oil

About 12 spicy tortilla chips

Bean puree with anchovies or smoked oysters

Improvise this first course from food you have in the pantry. I've given two possibilities here: you can top the seasoned puree of white beans with anchovy fillets or smoked oysters or mussels. Use your imagination to flavor the puree with what's on hand, from capers to pickles to sardines. Instead of white beans, you can use black beans, pinto beans, or chickpeas. ❧ *4 servings*

Put the cannellini beans in a food processor and add the garlic, olive oil, Tabasco, salt, and vinegar. Process until smooth, then transfer to a bowl. (You should have about 1½ cups.) Mix in the scallion. Set aside at room temperature.

For the garnish: Heat the oven to 400 degrees. Toss the bread cubes with the oil and toast on a cookie sheet for 8 to 10 minutes. Set aside.

At serving time, divide the bean puree among four plates and sprinkle the croutons and olives on top. Arrange the anchovy fillets on top of the croutons and sprinkle with cilantro, or top with the smoked mussels or oysters and, using a vegetable peeler, shave a few slices of radish on top.

1 can (about 18 ounces) cannellini beans, drained

2 small garlic cloves, peeled and crushed

2 tablespoons good olive oil

½ teaspoon Tabasco sauce

½ teaspoon salt

1 teaspoon sherry vinegar

2 tablespoons finely minced scallion

Garnish

2 slices country bread (2 ounces), cut into ½-inch dice (about 1 cup)

1 tablespoon peanut or canola oil

About 20 oil-cured black olives, pitted

About 3 flat anchovies in oil (from a 2-ounce can), or 4 or 5 smoked oysters or mussels (from a 3½-ounce can)

A few fresh cilantro leaves or 1 radish

White bean and sardine toasts

Experiment and make these delicious snacks your own. You can use red or white beans, chickpeas, or limas. I like the assertive taste of cilantro, but the toasts are also good with parsley, tarragon, chives, or basil. Slices of baguette or rolls can be substituted for the country bread. If using the bread, make serving easier by cutting it into manageable slices before spreading the beans on top. Instead of anchovies and sardines, you can make the salad with canned tuna or salmon.

This dish loves oil, particularly the best extra-virgin olive oil; you might sprinkle on a few more drops at serving time.

4 servings

1 can (14 ½ ounces) cannellini beans, drained and rinsed under warm running water

½ teaspoon chopped garlic

⅓ cup finely chopped onion

½ teaspoon salt

½ teaspoon freshly ground black pepper

¼ cup extra-virgin olive oil

4 anchovy fillets, cut into ½-inch pieces

1 can (3¾ ounces) sardines in oil (about 4 sardines), drained and broken into 1-inch pieces

For serving

1 tablespoon extra-virgin olive oil, plus more for serving if desired

1 thick slice (¾ inch) from a country bread loaf (about 8 inches in diameter and weighing about 6 ounces)

¼ cup (loosely packed) fresh cilantro or flat-leaf parsley leaves

Put the beans in a bowl with the garlic, onion, salt, pepper, olive oil, anchovies, and sardines. Toss gently to mix and set aside, or cover and refrigerate until about 15 minutes before serving time.

To serve, heat the oven to 400 degrees. Spread the olive oil on a cookie sheet. Lightly press the bread slice into the oil to coat it on one side, then turn it over and press lightly again so both sides of the bread are coated with oil. Bake for 10 to 12 minutes, until nicely browned, then transfer to a platter. Cut the toasted bread into 4 wedges and re-form it into a slice on the platter.

Heat the bean mixture in a microwave oven for about 1 minute to warm it slightly, then spread it on the bread. Sprinkle the cilantro or parsley on top and serve with additional olive oil, if you like.

Devil shrimp

I like my shrimp spicy. These are best served in informal settings, since you'll want to suck on the shrimp to extract all their tangy goodness before peeling them with your fingers and eating them. *4 servings*

Put all the ingredients in a saucepan and mix well. Cover and bring to a boil, which should take about 3 minutes, stirring occasionally. As soon as the mixture boils, set the pan aside off the heat, still covered, for 10 minutes. Transfer the shrimp and sauce to a serving bowl and serve at room temperature, or cool and refrigerate for serving later, either cool or at room temperature.

1 pound raw shrimp in shells (30–40)

3 tablespoons ketchup

2 tablespoons good olive oil

2 tablespoons hot chili sauce or Asian chili paste

1 tablespoon chopped garlic

1 cup thinly sliced scallions (about 6 scallions)

½ teaspoon salt

⅓ cup water

Chopped chicken livers with spinach salad

When my wife, Gloria, was in high school, she sometimes went to her friend Hindell's house. The family's housekeeper taught her how to make this chopped chicken liver, and it's been a favorite ever since. Instead of mounding it on the salad, you can serve it lukewarm or cold on thin wheat crackers.

The key to this recipe is the chicken (or duck) fat, which is highly flavorful. You can render the chicken fat yourself or buy commercial schmaltz (rendered chicken fat), which is available in most supermarkets.

4 servings (about 2 cups)

For the chicken livers: Cut the chicken or duck fat into ¼-inch pieces and melt it in a skillet over medium heat. Add the livers, onions, salt, and pepper, heat over high heat for about 1 minute, then reduce the heat to medium, cover, and cook for 10 minutes.

Pour the contents of the skillet into a sieve set over a bowl so that any liquefied fat will drip into the bowl. When the solids in

Chicken livers

About 3 ounces chicken fat or duck fat

8 ounces chicken livers

2 cups sliced onions (about 10 ounces)

¾ teaspoon salt

½ teaspoon freshly ground black pepper

3 hard-cooked large eggs, peeled

Thin wheat crackers, for serving

Spinach salad

4 cups (loosely packed) baby spinach leaves, washed and dried

1 tablespoon good olive oil

1 teaspoon red wine vinegar

Kosher salt and freshly ground black pepper

½ cup Multipurpose Herbed Crumbs (page 81; optional)

the sieve are cool enough to handle, transfer them to a cutting board and chop coarsely with a knife. Return the chopped mixture to the bowl containing the fat.

Using an egg slicer, cut an egg into slices, then pivot the slices together 90 degrees in the slicer and slice it again; chop it coarsely with a knife. Repeat with the remaining eggs, add the cut eggs to the liver in the bowl, and mix well. The chicken livers can be stored in the refrigerator for up to a week.

For the spinach salad: Toss the spinach with the oil, vinegar, and dash of salt and pepper. Divide among four plates.

Spoon ⅓ to ½ cup of the chopped livers into the center of each salad. Sprinkle with the herbed crumbs, if you like, and serve.

About chicken fat

I pull the loose fat from the cavity of a chicken and freeze it to keep on hand for this dish. To render chicken fat, cut it into small pieces and cook them in a small saucepan over low heat. Most of the fat will render out, but you will also have some small browned bits that you can add to the livers if you wish. You can do the same thing with duck fat.

◄← MAKE AHEAD
The chopped chicken livers can be made 1 to 2 days ahead.

Toasted bread and mozzarella

This fast and easy dish made with ingredients that I always have at home pleases everyone. Mozzarella can be replaced with a Swiss cheese, such as Gruyère, or with Cheddar. Be sure to use a gratin dish or shallow baking dish large enough to hold the slices of bread in one layer without overlapping.

4 servings

2½ tablespoons good olive oil

About 16 slices (each ½ inch thick) from a baguette

About 6 ounces mozzarella cheese, cut into 16 slices

About 16 garlic flakes (thin slices removed with a vegetable peeler from 2–3 cloves)

¼ teaspoon salt

½ teaspoon freshly ground black pepper

About 1 dozen whole oil-cured black olives, pitted

Heat the oven to 425 degrees. Pour 1½ tablespoons of the oil into a gratin dish or shallow baking dish, and spread evenly to coat the bottom of the dish. Arrange the bread slices on top in one layer, press to coat them on one side with the oil, then turn them over and arrange them again in one layer in the dish so that they are oiled on both sides. Arrange a slice of cheese and a garlic flake on top of each slice of bread, then sprinkle on the salt and pepper and drizzle with the remaining 1 tablespoon oil.

Bake the gratin for 8 to 10 minutes, until the cheese is melted and lightly browned on top. Sprinkle the olives on top and serve.

Sweet cheese medley

Here's a great recipe to make when you have several different kinds of leftover cheese. This mixture will keep for a couple of weeks in the refrigerator, so you can have it on hand for surprise guests.

Be sure to trim off any mold or dry crust from the cheese.

≈ *about 30 appetizers*

½ pound assorted cheeses (I like a mixture of Gloucester, feta, blue, Gouda, and Gruyère)

⅓ cup pumpkin seeds

⅓ cup dark raisins

⅓ cup honey

2 tablespoons fresh lime juice

¾ teaspoon freshly ground black pepper

Salt, if needed

About 30 thin wheat crackers

About 30 mint or spearmint leaves

Cut or crumble the cheese into about ½-inch pieces and put them in a bowl. Toast the pumpkin seeds in a skillet over medium to high heat for 3 to 4 minutes, stirring occasionally. Add to the cheese in the bowl, along with the raisins, honey, lime juice, and pepper. Mix well, taste for salt (some cheese is salty), and add salt, if needed.

Mound a heaping teaspoon of the cheese medley on each of the crackers, stick a mint leaf on top, and serve.

Two spicy salsas

Any bland dish can be awakened with a few tablespoons of salsa. In addition to enjoying salsa as a snack, I use it in salad dressing, in sauces for fish or meat, and even in soups and stews. Fresh salsa, often found near the hot chile peppers in the supermarket's produce section, is a great convenience, but your own will be even better.

It's important to rinse the chopped onion under cold running water to prevent discoloration and keep the onion from tasting too strong in the finished dish.

Red hot salsa

❧ *2½ cups*

Mix all the ingredients together in a bowl. Cover and refrigerate for up to 2 weeks.

2 cups diced (½-inch) tomatoes, including skin and seeds

¼ cup minced jalapeño or serrano pepper (more or less, depending on your tolerance)

⅓ cup coarsely chopped onion, put in a sieve and rinsed under cold running water

⅓ cup coarsely chopped fresh cilantro

1 tablespoon finely chopped garlic

½ teaspoon salt

2 tablespoons fresh lime juice

3 tablespoons ketchup

2 tablespoons water

Green hot salsa

≈ 2 cups

Mix all the ingredients together in a bowl. Cover and refrigerate for up to 2 weeks.

About hot peppers

Whether you decide to use jalapeño, serrano, poblano, or the fiery habanero chiles, taste a tiny bit as you cut them, because the hotness varies from one to another of the same variety. Add just as much to the dish as you can tolerate. If you want, remove the seeds; that's where much of the heat is.

1½ cups diced (½-inch) tomatillos (about 8 ounces; 3 or 4, depending on size)

½ cup minced scallions

1½ tablespoons finely chopped garlic

⅓ cup finely diced poblano pepper, or another variety to your liking

½ cup coarsely chopped fresh cilantro

2 tablespoons fresh lime juice

½ teaspoon kosher salt

2 tablespoons water

Melon and prosciutto

Melon and prosciutto is a classic first course, excellent as a summer starter. Depending on the quality of the melon and the ham, this dish can be great or ordinary. I favor muskmelons, known as cantaloupes in the United States. Sometimes, at Connecticut farm markets, I can find the French cantaloupe, the charentais, of which there are many types, some with netted and some with smooth skin, including the Cavaillon. My favorite ham is the Spanish Serrano, shaved very thin. Parma ham (prosciutto) is also excellent. Both are available at good delicatessens and specialty markets.

❧ *4 servings*

1 ripe melon (about 1¾ pounds)
4 teaspoons fresh lemon juice
½ teaspoon coarse salt (preferably *fleur de sel*)
¾ teaspoon coarsely ground black pepper
3–4 ounces thinly shaved prosciutto or Serrano ham

Using a paring knife, peel the melon as you would an apple, removing the outer skin and any green parts underneath. Cut a slice from the melon to expose the seeds, then remove them. Cut the melon into 1½-inch pieces. (You should have about 4 cups.)

At serving time, put 1 cup of the melon pieces on each of four plates. Sprinkle each serving with 1 teaspoon of the lemon juice, and divide the salt and pepper among the individual servings. Drape the prosciutto over the melon and serve immediately.

About melons

Make sure that you buy a ripe melon. It should be heavy and fragrant.

Soups

Instant vegetable soup

It couldn't be easier or faster to prepare this soup. Gloria calls it "fridge soup," because I make it with whatever left-over vegetables I have in the refrigerator. In the time it takes to bring the water to a boil, I can usually shred the vegetables for the soup. (I use the large-holed side of a box grater.)

Instead of using the vegetables here, I have also made this soup with broccoli, cauliflower, cabbage, eggplant, and potatoes. I like to thicken it with a starch and sometimes add angel hair pasta, semolina, oatmeal, yellow cornmeal, or tapioca instead. Experiment—it will become your soup. A dash of butter or oil is a nice finishing touch, with some shredded Gruyère cheese added at the table.

When I was a child, my mother used to add cold milk to our soup, and I still love it that way. ⟿ *4 servings*

5 cups water
1½ cups shredded zucchini (about half a zucchini)
1 cup shredded peeled carrot (about 1 carrot)
1 cup shredded onion (1 medium onion)
1 cup shredded white button mushrooms (2–4 mushrooms)
⅓ cup minced scallions (about 3 scallions)
2 cups (loosely packed) coarsely chopped salad greens
1 teaspoon salt
3 tablespoons instant grits
About 4 teaspoons unsalted butter or olive oil
1 cup shredded Swiss (Gruyère) cheese

Bring the water to a boil in a large saucepan. Add all the vegetables to the boiling water along with the salt. Bring the soup back to a boil and boil, uncovered, for 2 to 3 minutes. Sprinkle the grits on top of the soup, reduce the heat to low, and cook gently for 2 to 3 minutes longer. (You will have about 6 cups.)

Serve hot in soup bowls, spooning about 1 teaspoon of the olive oil or butter on each serving and topping each of the bowls with a few generous tablespoonfuls of the cheese.

Pumpkin soup with toasted walnuts

When I was a kid in France, pumpkin was used in savory gratins or soups but never in sweet desserts. Over the years, I have learned to love pumpkin pie, though I still use this favorite vegetable in soups.

The pumpkin puree available in cans consists of pumpkin and a dash of salt and is excellent when you need a quick first course.

4 servings

Heat the oil in a large saucepan over medium heat and add the onion, celery, and garlic. Cook, stirring occasionally, for about 2 minutes to soften the vegetables. Add the chicken stock, salt, and pepper, and bring to a boil. Boil for 6 to 8 minutes, then stir in the pumpkin puree. Mix well, bring back to a boil, and boil for 5 minutes. Emulsify with a hand blender or in a food processor until smooth.

At serving time, reheat the soup and stir in the butter. Mix well to incorporate. (You will have about 6 cups.) Serve in soup bowls with a heaping tablespoon of sour cream in the centers, and 5 toasted walnuts and a sprinkling of chives on top of each serving.

◂+ MAKE AHEAD

Once you've emulsified the soup, it can be cooled, covered, and refrigerated for a few days.

1½ tablespoons good olive oil

1 cup coarsely chopped onion

1 cup coarsely chopped celery

2 garlic cloves, peeled and crushed

4 cups chicken stock, homemade (see page 55), or low-salt canned chicken broth

About ¾ teaspoon salt (less if using canned chicken broth)

½ teaspoon freshly ground black pepper

1 (15-ounce) can pumpkin puree

1½ tablespoons unsalted butter

About ½ cup sour cream

20 walnut halves, sprinkled with a dash of salt and cayenne pepper and toasted on a cookie sheet for 10 minutes in a 350-degree oven

1 tablespoon minced fresh chives

Silky tomato soup with spinach coulis

This refreshing summer soup, a silky blend of raw tomato flavored with garlic and oil, is almost a liquid salad. It's excellent on its own, but when garnished with a simple spinach coulis, or puree, it is sublime.

The spinach puree is an excellent addition to sandwiches or soups and is great as a dressing for cold poached fish or as a sauce for pasta. ❧ *4 servings*

For the tomato soup: Cut the tomatoes into 2- to 3-inch chunks. Finely puree the tomatoes, onion, garlic, jalapeño, salt, and olive oil in a blender or food processor. Push the puree through a food mill fitted with the fine screen, then add enough Tabasco to the soup to suit your taste. (You should have about 6 cups of soup.) Refrigerate until cool.

For the spinach coulis: Pick out and discard any damaged leaves and seal the leaves in a plastic bag. Place the bag in a microwave oven and microwave the spinach on high for 1½ minutes.

Transfer the spinach to a blender. Add the oil, salt, and water and process for about 1 minute, stopping the machine once or twice to push any pieces of spinach clinging to the sides down into the mixture. When it's smooth, transfer the spinach puree to a bottle or jar, cover tightly, and refrigerate.

To serve, ladle out about 1½ cups soup per person. Garnish each bowl with 1 to 2 tablespoons of spinach coulis.

◄**+ MAKE AHEAD**

The spinach coulis can be made up to a week ahead and refrigerated.

Tomato soup

- 3 pounds ripe tomatoes
- 1 sweet onion (about 4 ounces), such as Vidalia, cut into 1-inch pieces
- 2 large garlic cloves
- ¼ jalapeño pepper (or less, depending on your tolerance), seeded and cut into ½-inch pieces
- ¾ teaspoon salt
- 2 tablespoons good olive oil
- ¼ teaspoon (or less, if desired) Tabasco sauce

Spinach coulis

- About 3 cups (loosely packed) spinach leaves
- ¼ cup oil (a mixture of canola and olive oil)
- ¼ teaspoon salt
- ¼ cup water

Mushroom velouté with almonds

This simple velouté (meaning velvety) is made with regular white button mushrooms. They have a wonderful flavor—especially as they get older and their gills begin to open.

A piece of dried tree ear mushroom, commonly used in Chinese cooking, is added to the soup for extra flavor, then removed and used as a garnish for serving. (Dried tree ears can be found in Asian markets and in many supermarkets.)

A sprinkling of browned sliced almonds lends a delightful crunch. ❧ *4 servings*

Heat the butter in a saucepan over medium heat and add the shallots and garlic. Cook for about 2 minutes, or until softened. Add the flour and stir well. Stir in the stock, salt, and pepper, and bring to a boil.

Meanwhile, wash the button mushrooms and chop them coarsely. (You should have about 7 cups.) Add them to the stock with the dried tree ear mushroom. Bring back to a boil, reduce the heat

<table>
<tr><td>2</td><td>tablespoons unsalted butter</td></tr>
<tr><td>1</td><td>cup sliced shallots</td></tr>
<tr><td>1</td><td>tablespoon sliced garlic</td></tr>
<tr><td>1½</td><td>tablespoons all-purpose flour</td></tr>
<tr><td>4</td><td>cups chicken stock, homemade (see page 55), or low-salt canned chicken broth</td></tr>
<tr><td></td><td>About ¾ teaspoon salt (less if using canned chicken broth)</td></tr>
<tr><td>¼</td><td>teaspoon freshly ground black pepper</td></tr>
<tr><td>1</td><td>pound white button mushrooms (preferably older ones with open gills)</td></tr>
<tr><td>1–2</td><td>pieces dried tree ear mushroom (also known as wood ear and cloud ear mushroom)</td></tr>
<tr><td>⅓</td><td>cup sliced almonds</td></tr>
<tr><td>1</td><td>cup half-and-half</td></tr>
</table>

to low, and simmer, partially covered, for 30 minutes; remove the tree ear mushroom after 10 minutes. When it is cool enough to handle, remove and discard any tough roots from the tree ear and chop it coarsely. (You should have about ¼ cup.)

Sauté the almonds in a small, nonstick saucepan over medium heat for 2 to 3 minutes stirring often, until they are lightly toasted. Take them out of the pan immediately.

When the soup is cooked, emulsify it until smooth with a hand blender or in a food processor. At serving time, add the half-and-half to the soup and bring it back to a boil. (You will have about 6 cups.) Divide among four soup bowls, and serve hot with a sprinkling of the tree ear mushroom and sliced almonds on top.

Corn and hominy chowder

I find the taste of hominy addictive. I always keep a few cans in my pantry. One day I decided to include it in this fast and flavorful soup. It was a hit!   ❧ *6 servings*

Heat the oil in a large saucepan over medium heat and add the garlic, onion, and scallions. Cook for 3 minutes, then add the rest of the ingredients, except for the corn and cilantro. Bring to a boil, and cook for 15 minutes. Stir in the corn and cilantro, return to a boil, and serve.

3 tablespoons good olive oil

1½ tablespoons chopped garlic

1 cup chopped onion

½ cup minced scallions

½ cup Green Hot Salsa (page 41), or less for a milder soup

1 (14-ounce) can diced tomatoes in sauce

1 (28-ounce) can white hominy (about 3 cups kernels and juice)

½ teaspoon ground cinnamon

2 teaspoons ground cumin

½ teaspoon dried thyme leaves

4 cups chicken stock, homemade (see page 55), or low-salt canned chicken broth

About ½ teaspoon salt (less if using canned chicken broth)

1½ cups corn kernels (from 2 ears corn)

½ cup (lightly packed) fresh cilantro, finely chopped

Lobster bisque

Prepared in the classic way, this flavorful and inexpensive bisque is made from the broth and lobster bodies from Lobster Salad with Tarragon (page 31). If your fishmonger can get you two lobster bodies, however, make the bisque with them or with the frozen bodies of lobsters you served during the summer. ❧ *4 servings*

2 tablespoons good olive oil

Reserved lobster bodies and broth (about 3 cups) from Lobster Salad with Tarragon (page 31)

1 cup coarsely chopped celery

1 cup coarsely chopped onion

4 unpeeled garlic cloves, crushed

¾ cup dry white wine

2 tablespoons all-purpose flour

2 tablespoons tomato paste

2 fresh thyme sprigs

2 teaspoons coarsely chopped fresh tarragon

¼ teaspoon cayenne pepper

Salt, if needed

¼ cup heavy cream

1 tablespoon good cognac

1 tablespoon minced fresh chives

Heat the olive oil in a large saucepan over medium heat and add the lobster body pieces. Cook, stirring occasionally, for 6 to 8 minutes, until the pieces start to brown. Stir in the celery, onion, and garlic and cook the mixture gently for 5 minutes, or until the vegetables are soft. Mix the wine and flour together until smooth in a measuring cup.

Add the wine mixture, reserved lobster broth, tomato paste, thyme, tarragon, and cayenne to the saucepan and bring the mixture to a boil. Cover, reduce the heat to low, and boil gently for 10 to 15 minutes. Drain in a colander set over a bowl, pressing with a spoon to extract as much juice as possible. Strain the stock through a fine sieve into a saucepan. (You should have 3 to 4 cups; add water if necessary.) Taste and add salt, if needed.

At serving time, add the cream and cognac to the stock and heat until the bisque comes to a boil. Sprinkle with chives and serve immediately.

◄← MAKE AHEAD

You can prepare the stock and freeze it. Finish the bisque with the last-minute addition of cream, cognac, and chives.

Basic chicken stock

When I have a spare moment on the weekend, I make this salt-free stock, defat it, and then freeze it in two-cup batches in plastic zipper-lock bags. The stock takes a little time to simmer, but the result is well worth the time and effort. You can use either uncooked chicken or turkey bones or, if you have roasted a bird, make the stock with the roasted bones. ⟿ *2½ quarts (10 cups)*

3 pounds chicken or turkey bones and parts (necks and backs, skinless or with as little skin as possible, and gizzards)

6 quarts lukewarm water

1 teaspoon dried thyme leaves

4 bay leaves
About ½ teaspoon whole cloves

1 large onion (about 8 ounces), peeled and quartered

1 teaspoon celery seed

1 tablespoon dark soy sauce

Bring the bones, chicken parts, and water to a boil in a large stockpot over high heat. Reduce the heat to low and boil the mixture gently for 30 minutes. Most of the fat and impurities will rise to the surface during this time; skim off as much as you can.

Add the remaining ingredients, return the liquid to a boil, then boil very gently over low heat, partially covered, for 2 hours. Strain the liquid through a fine-mesh sieve or a colander lined with a dampened kitchen towel or dampened paper towels.

Allow the stock to cool. Remove the surface fat and freeze the stock in plastic zipper-lock bags. Use as needed.

About chicken stock

If you don't have time in your schedule to make homemade stock, feel free to substitute low-salt canned chicken broth for chicken stock in the recipes in this book. If you do so, however, remember that all canned broth contains some salt, so adjust the recipes accordingly.

Eggs

Scrambled eggs with mushrooms and truffles

I prepare these eggs as they would be made in the South of France. Seasoned with shallots and mushrooms, they are perfumed with truffles for serving as an elegant first course. If you can't find good truffles, substitute good truffle oil, which you can find in specialty stores. Organic eggs are far superior to supermarket eggs. Use them whenever possible.

≈ 4 servings

Using a whisk, beat the eggs in a medium bowl with the salt, pepper, chives, and sour cream for a minute or so, until fluffy and well mixed.

Heat the butter and oil in a nonstick skillet over medium heat. Add the shallots and mushrooms and cook for about 3 minutes, or until tender.

Meanwhile, arrange the lettuce cups in four soup plates. Mix the olive oil, garlic, and salt in a small bowl and dab it onto the leaves.

Add the egg mixture to the mushrooms in the skillet and cook over medium heat, stirring with a spoon or rubber spatula, for 2 to 3 minutes, until the mixture is set but still a bit runny.

To serve, divide the eggs among the lettuce cups. Scatter the truffle shavings on top, or drizzle with the truffle oil.

8 large eggs (preferably organic)
½ teaspoon salt
½ teaspoon freshly ground black pepper
2 tablespoons minced fresh chives
⅓ cup sour cream
1 tablespoon unsalted butter
1 tablespoon good olive oil
⅓ cup chopped shallots
2 cups diced (½-inch) white button mushrooms (about 4 ounces)

Garnish

4–8 Boston lettuce leaves (for use as cups to hold the eggs)
1 tablespoon extra-virgin olive oil
½ teaspoon finely chopped garlic
Dash of salt

1 black truffle, sliced with a vegetable peeler into thin shavings, or 2 tablespoons truffle oil

Scrambled eggs on tomato jus

Ideal as a main course for lunch or a first course for dinner, these scrambled eggs are served warm in a cool tomato *jus*. I flavor the eggs with bacon, scallions, and cheese here, but herbs, sausages, ham, or mushrooms work very well as variations. ⤙ *4 servings*

For the tomato jus*:* Cut the tomato into pieces and push it through a food mill. (You should have about ⅔ cup juice; add water, if necessary.) Pour the juice into a bowl, add the oil and salt, and mix well with a whisk to emulsify. Set aside.

For the scrambled eggs: Scatter the bacon pieces in a nonstick skillet and cook over medium-high heat until crisp, 1½ to 2 minutes. Add the scallions and cook for 10 seconds.

Break the eggs into a bowl and add the salt and pepper. Beat well with a fork. Add to the hot skillet and cook over medium heat, stirring with a wooden or rubber spatula, until the eggs are set but still a bit runny. Scrape the eggs into a bowl and stir in the cheese. Set aside until ready to serve. (The eggs should be served lukewarm.)

At serving time, divide the *jus* among four plates. Divide the eggs among the plates, either spooning them into a mound on the *jus* in the centers of the plates or into a ring mold 2 to 3 inches in diameter and about 1½ inches deep (a tuna fish can with both ends removed works well). Place the mold in the center of one of the plates, mound the eggs inside, then remove the ring gently. Repeat this procedure on the other plates to create four mounds. Garnish with the chives and serve immediately.

Tomato jus

- 1 large ripe tomato (about 6 ounces)
- 2 tablespoons good olive oil
- ¼ teaspoon salt

Scrambled eggs

- 3 slices bacon, cut into ½-inch pieces
- ¼ cup minced scallions
- 8 large eggs (preferably organic)
- ¼ teaspoon salt
- ¼ teaspoon freshly ground black pepper
- ½ cup grated Swiss (Gruyère or Emmenthaler) cheese
- 1 tablespoon minced fresh chives

About scrambled eggs

Be sure to keep the scrambled eggs moist. If you overcook them, add a couple of tablespoons of cold milk to the skillet to stop the cooking and moisten the eggs.

Egg and tomato gratin

When I was a child, we ate eggs more often than meat; they were economical and nutritious, and I remember these dishes with fondness. We rarely eat eggs for breakfast at our house now but enjoy them in gratins like this one, which we serve as a first course or light lunch.

The recipe, intended to serve four, uses six eggs, which means that each person consumes only 1½ eggs. The sauce is also lean. Although it can be made with fresh tomatoes when they are at their best, I often use canned tomatoes instead, because they're more flavorful, more colorful, and less expensive during much of the year. ❧ *4 servings*

Poke the rounded end of each egg with a pushpin to help prevent it from cracking, and lower the eggs into a saucepan of boiling water to cover. Bring the water back to a boil, then boil the eggs very gently for 10 minutes. Drain and cool in ice water for at least 15 minutes, or until the centers of the eggs are completely cool. Peel the eggs and cut each of them into 6 wedges.

6 large eggs (preferably organic)

2 tablespoons good olive oil

2 medium onions (about 12 ounces), sliced (about 2½ cups)

4 teaspoons chopped garlic

¾ teaspoon dried thyme leaves

½ teaspoon salt

½ teaspoon freshly ground black pepper

1 (14-ounce) can peeled tomatoes

⅔ cup grated Swiss (Gruyère or Emmenthaler) or mozzarella cheese (2½ ounces)

Arrange the wedges in a 6-cup-capacity gratin dish or baking dish.

Heat the oven to 400 degrees. Heat the oil in a skillet over medium-high heat until hot but not smoking. Add the onions and sauté for about 2 minutes, then add the garlic, thyme, salt, and pepper. Crush the tomatoes into pieces and add them along with their juice to the skillet. Bring the mixture to a boil, reduce the heat, and boil gently, covered, for 4 minutes.

Pour the onion and tomato mixture over the eggs in the gratin dish and sprinkle the cheese on top. Bake the gratin for 10 minutes.

Meanwhile, heat the broiler. When the gratin is cooked, broil 3 to 4 inches from the heat source for 2 to 3 minutes to brown the top. Serve.

About hard-cooked eggs

It's important to cook eggs properly. Pricking them before cooking helps relieve the pressure created in the air chamber surrounding the whites of the eggs as they are placed in the boiling water. Air bubbles will emerge, and the eggs will be much less likely to break.

Lower the eggs into boiling water and cook them at a very gentle boil; rapid boiling toughens them. After 10 minutes, drain off the water and shake the pan to crack the eggshells. Cover the eggs with cold water and ice and leave them in the ice water long enough to cool completely inside. This technique prevents the exterior of the yolks from turning green, eliminates the strong smell of sulfur and ensures that they will be perfectly cooked.

-←- MAKE AHEAD

The dish can be assembled up to a couple of hours ahead, refrigerated, and finished in the oven. Allow 20 minutes for baking the gratin if it is cold when placed in the oven.

Bow-tie pasta with fried eggs and cheese

This is truly one of my favorite dishes to eat at home. Gloria and I like our pasta simply seasoned with the best possible olive oil, salt, pepper, chives, and Gruyère cheese, which melts from the heat of the pasta. Make sure that the serving plates—we use soup plates—are very hot.

If you want, use just one egg per serving. ❧ *4 servings*

12 ounces bow-tie (farfalle) pasta (about 6 cups)

¼ cup extra-virgin olive oil

2 tablespoons minced fresh chives

½ teaspoon salt

½ teaspoon freshly ground black pepper

Garnish

2 tablespoons unsalted butter

8 large eggs (preferably organic)

About 1⅓ cups grated Swiss (Gruyère or Emmenthaler) cheese (7 ounces)

Bring 3 quarts salted water to a boil. Add the pasta to the boiling water and cook for about 12 minutes, or until it is done to your liking.

Meanwhile, put the olive oil, chives, salt, and pepper in a bowl large enough to hold the cooked pasta. When the pasta is ready, remove ½ cup of the cooking water and add it to the bowl. Drain the pasta well, add it to the bowl, and toss well.

For the garnish: Melt ½ tablespoon of the butter in each of two 6-inch nonstick skillets. Break 2 of the eggs into each skillet and cook, covered, over medium-high heat for about 2 minutes, or just until the whites are set. Spoon a 6-ounce ladle of pasta into each of two warmed soup plates and sprinkle on a heaping spoonful of cheese. Place the 2 eggs on top of the pasta, add a little more cheese, then a half ladle of pasta. (The egg yolks should still be visible through the top layer of pasta.) Cook the remaining 4 eggs and assemble the two remaining plates in the same way. Serve immediately.

To warm dinner plates

We all know that hot food stays hot much longer when served on warmed plates. My good friend Jean-Claude Szurdak tells me that just before plating the food, he microwaves a stack of as many plates (usually four to six) as he needs for the meal on high for 1½ to 2 minutes.

Salads

Summer salad

My tastes run mostly to simple green salads, but I enjoy combining many ingredients, so I often make this salad, or a similar one (depending on what's available) during the summer when tomatoes are ripe. ❧ *4 servings*

Combine all the ingredients except the Boston lettuce in a large salad bowl. Arrange a lettuce leaf on each of four plates and divide the salad among the plates, spooning it into the lettuce leaves. Serve immediately.

1⅓ cups diced (1-inch) peeled and seeded cucumber

1⅓ cups diced (1-inch) ripe tomato

⅓ cup sliced (1-inch) scallions

¾ cup diced (½-inch) sweet onion, such as Vidalia

½ cup spicy green pitted olives, halved if large

3 tablespoons extra-virgin olive oil

1 tablespoon red wine vinegar

¾ teaspoon salt

½ teaspoon freshly ground black pepper

1 tablespoon fresh tarragon leaves

4 large Boston lettuce leaves, washed and dried

Romaine and radicchio with salsa dressing

Serve this excellent salad as a first course or as an accompaniment to roasted poultry, meat, or even fish. The secret ingredient is hot salsa, which is combined with balsamic vinegar, cilantro, and olive oil to produce a fragrant, piquant dressing.

Treviso is a type of radicchio, the burgundy red winter salad green with firm, slightly bitter leaves. The more familiar Verona radicchio grows in tight round heads, while Treviso has narrow, elongated leaves, like Belgian endive. If Treviso is not available, substitute Verona radicchio.

4 servings

Salsa dressing

- ¼ cup Red Hot Salsa (page 41) or fresh store-bought salsa
- 2 tablespoons extra-virgin olive oil
- 1½ teaspoons balsamic vinegar
- ½ teaspoon salt
- ¼ cup (loosely packed) fresh cilantro leaves
- 6 cups (loosely packed) 2-inch pieces romaine lettuce and Treviso radicchio, washed and dried

Mix all the dressing ingredients together in a salad bowl.

At serving time, add the mixed salad greens and toss well. Serve.

Coleslaw

I learned how to make coleslaw when I worked at Howard Johnson's, and it has been part of my repertoire ever since. Particularly in summer, I serve it with roasts, grilled steaks, and chicken, as well as with lobster rolls and broiled fish.

I cut the cabbage by hand, but a food processor fitted with a shredding disk or a conventional box grater works well for shredding the cabbage and carrot.

When I can find large black radishes—which look like black turnips   I grate one on a box grater and add it to my slaw to lend some heat and a special taste. Sometimes I add minced chives or grated onion.   ❧ *6 to 8 servings*

About 10 cups shredded cabbage (from 1 head cabbage, about 2 pounds)
1 cup shredded carrot
1 cup mayonnaise
⅓ cup apple cider vinegar
2 teaspoons poppy seeds
1½ teaspoons sugar
1¼ teaspoons salt
½ teaspoon Tabasco sauce

Mix all the ingredients together thoroughly in a bowl and refrigerate until ready to serve.

◂ **MAKE AHEAD**

I like this coleslaw best when it's made about 3 hours ahead; the cabbage softens a little while remaining crunchy. When kept longer, it renders some liquid, but it will keep well, refrigerated, for at least 2 days.

Zucchini and tomato salad

For this recipe, I salt long, thin strips of zucchini and serve them raw. The salt flavors the zucchini and draws out its moisture, giving it a deliciously crunchy texture. Sometimes I serve the zucchini on its own with just a dash of olive oil, but it's also wonderful with this tomato, mozzarella, and cilantro salad, which can be served on its own.

4 servings

Using a vegetable peeler, cut down the length of each zucchini to remove long, thin strips. Stop when you reach the seeds in the center, pivot the zucchini, and repeat on the other 3 sides. Discard the seedy centers and put the zucchini strips in a nonreactive bowl. Sprinkle with ½ teaspoon of the salt, mix well, and set aside until serving time.

In another bowl, mix together the tomatoes, mozzarella, cilantro, lemon juice, oil, the remaining ½ teaspoon salt, and the pepper.

At serving time, arrange the zucchini strips on four plates to create a border around the edge. Spoon some of the tomato salad into the center of each plate and serve immediately.

2 small, firm zucchini (each about 5 ounces)

1 teaspoon salt

2 cups diced (¾-inch) tomatoes

⅔ cup diced (½-inch) mozzarella cheese, preferably buffalo mozzarella

About ½ cup (loosely packed) fresh cilantro leaves

2 tablespoons fresh lemon juice

¼ cup extra-virgin olive oil

½ teaspoon freshly ground black pepper

◄+ MAKE AHEAD

Both the zucchini and the tomato salad can be prepared up to 2 hours ahead of serving; if done any further ahead, they both tend to get mushy.

Parsley and pumpkin seed salad

My father liked parsley and used it in everything; he told us that it was good for the blood. Well, this assertive, highly seasoned parsley salad—one of our summer favorites—will certainly wake you up, even though the elephant garlic it contains is fairly mild. Save the parsley stems for stock.   ❧ *4 servings*

Put the parsley leaves in a medium bowl. Cut the anchovy fillets into ½-inch pieces and add them to the bowl, along with the carrot, salt, pepper, and olive oil. Using a vegetable peeler, cut the garlic clove into thin flakes (you should have about ⅓ cup) and mix them with the ingredients in the bowl.

Lower the eggs into in a small saucepan of boiling water and boil gently for 10 minutes (see page 61). Drain, add ice and cold water to the pan, and cool thoroughly. Shell the eggs, cut into pieces in an egg slicer or with a sharp knife, and set aside in a small bowl.

Heat the oven to 400 degrees. Place the bread slice on a small cookie sheet and bake for about 12 minutes, or until nicely browned.

At serving time, cut the toasted bread into four equal pieces and reassemble the slice in the center of a platter. Spoon the salad on top of the toast and sprinkle the egg and pumpkin seeds on top. Serve within 15 minutes.

4 cups (loosely packed) fresh flat-leaf parsley leaves, washed and dried

1 (2-ounce) can flat anchovy fillets in oil, drained

1 cup peeled, grated carrot (about 1 carrot)

½ teaspoon salt

¼ teaspoon freshly ground black pepper

¼ cup extra-virgin olive oil

1 elephant garlic clove

2 large eggs

1 large slice round country bread (8–10 inches in diameter, ¾ inch thick, and weighing 4–5 ounces)

¼ cup pumpkin seeds, toasted on a cookie sheet in a 400-degree oven for 6–8 minutes

---

◄← **MAKE AHEAD**
The salad should be prepared a couple of hours ahead of serving to soften the parsley somewhat. It's even good the following day. Wait until just before serving to spoon it onto the toast.

Greens with quick cream dressing

This was one of my mother's favorite ways to dress a salad of Boston lettuce or, sometimes, fresh haricots verts. The cream contains less than half the calories of the oil needed in a conventional dressing. For best results, make it at the last moment. This dressing is so good that I often serve it as a sauce—sometimes with a little grated horseradish and fresh herbs added—for poached fish dishes (see Poached Tilapia with Herbed Cream Sauce, page 128).

⨿ 4 servings

Cream dressing

¼ cup heavy cream

¼ teaspoon salt

¼ teaspoon freshly ground
      black pepper

1½ teaspoons red wine vinegar

About 8 cups (loosely packed) young Boston lettuce, washed and dried

For the dressing: Just before serving, put the cream, salt, and pepper in a salad bowl and whip with a whisk for about 15 seconds, or just until frothy. Stir in the vinegar.

Add the lettuce, toss briefly, and serve immediately.

Note: If overwhipped, the dressing will thicken quickly after the vinegar addition. If it thickens too much, dilute it with 1 tablespoon water before tossing it with the lettuce.

Mushroom and walnut salad with sour cream dressing

Firm white button or cremini mushrooms are best for this raw mushroom salad. Combined with the other ingredients, the mushrooms will release enough moisture after 15 or 20 minutes to soften while retaining some texture.

4 servings

Combine the mushrooms in a bowl with the walnut pieces, sour cream, scallions, lemon juice, salt, and pepper. Cover and refrigerate until serving time.

When ready to serve, arrange the lettuce leaves in nests in four wide dessert bowls. Spoon the mushroom salad into the lettuce nests and serve immediately.

4 cups sliced mushrooms, preferably white button or cremini (about 12 ounces)

½ cup walnut pieces (about 10 walnuts)

⅔ cup sour cream

½ cup minced scallions

2 tablespoons fresh lemon juice

1 teaspoon salt

1 teaspoon freshly ground black pepper

8–12 Boston lettuce leaves, washed and dried

MAKE AHEAD
I like to assemble this salad about an hour before serving, but it can be prepared 5 to 6 hours ahead.

Asian eggplant salad

The soft eggplant flesh with its pungent dressing goes well with the crisp, spicy watercress. If watercress is not available, substitute arugula. *4 servings*

For the eggplant: Heat the oven to 400 degrees. Peel the eggplants and cut them into ¼-inch-thick lengthwise slices (about 20 slices). Spread the canola or peanut oil on one or two non-stick cookie sheets, then arrange the eggplant slices on top. Press lightly on the slices to coat them with the oil, then turn them over so that they are lightly oiled on both sides. Sprinkle the salt on top. Bake for 20 to 25 minutes, until the slices are soft and very lightly browned.

For the dressing: Mix all the ingredients together in a small bowl.

Spread the watercress on a large platter. Fold the eggplant slices in half or into thirds and arrange them on the watercress. Just before serving, pour the dressing over the eggplant and watercress. If you like, sprinkle on the bread crumbs and serve, dividing the salad among four plates.

Eggplant

- 2 small, firm eggplants (about 1¼ pounds total)
- 2 tablespoons canola or peanut oil
- ½ teaspoon salt

Asian dressing

- 2 tablespoons soy sauce
- 2 teaspoons chopped garlic
- 1 teaspoon sugar
- 1 tablespoon dark (Asian) sesame oil
- 2 tablespoons extra-virgin olive oil
- ¼ teaspoon Tabasco sauce

  About 8 cups (loosely packed) watercress, washed and dried
- ⅓ cup Multipurpose Herbed Crumbs (page 81; optional)

Tomato and mozzarella fans

A tomato salad with mozzarella and basil is certainly one of the highlights of summer at our house, especially when our own tomatoes are ripe and the basil in our garden is abundant. My recipe differs from the standard only in its presentation: I cut the tomatoes into slices from the top to the stem end, but stop short of cutting them all the way through and leave them still attached at the base of the tomato. Then I insert slices of mozzarella between the tomato slices so that each tomato resembles a beautiful red and white fan when spread open.

The tomatoes are best served at room temperature, garnished with red onion and basil leaves and drizzled with olive oil and sherry vinegar.　　　　　*4 servings*

4 large ripe tomatoes
(6–7 ounces each)
About ¾-pound piece
mozzarella cheese
⅔ cup diced (¼-inch)
red onion
About 12 fresh
basil leaves

Dressing

¼ cup extra-virgin olive oil
1½ tablespoons sherry vinegar or
red wine vinegar
¾ teaspoon salt
¾ teaspoon freshly ground
black pepper

Remove the core from each tomato. Place the tomatoes stem sides down on a cutting board and cut them vertically into ¼-inch-thick slices (6 to 8 slices per tomato), stopping about ½ inch from the base of each tomato, so that the slices are still attached at the stem end. Cut the mozzarella in half lengthwise, then into ¼-inch-thick slices, and insert a slice of mozzarella between the slices of tomato, creating a fan effect.

For the dressing: Mix all the ingredients together in a small bowl.

Arrange the tomatoes on a serving plate. Sprinkle with the diced onion and spoon some dressing on top so that it runs between the slices of tomato and mozzarella. Tear the basil leaves into pieces and scatter them around and on top of the tomatoes. Serve at room temperature.

Tomato tartare with tomato water sauce

A tartare is the name given to a dish of ground raw beef served with seasonings and herbs. My tomato tartare has the look of the original and is delightfully refreshing for a first course. For a sauce, I emulsify the tomato water (so called because it is the clear liquid squeezed from the tomato halves) with olive oil and garnish the dish with herbs—tarragon or chives. If you don't have enough tomato water for the sauce, add some tomato juice, Bloody Mary mix, or V8 juice. ❧ *4 servings*

For the tomato tartare: Cut the tomato in half and squeeze the halves into a sieve set over a bowl to release the seeds and juice. Press with a spoon to extract as much juice from the seeds as possible; set aside.

Cut the tomato flesh into ¾-inch pieces. (You will have about 1½ cups.) Put the tomato pieces in a bowl and add the seeds in the sieve to them. Add the remaining ingredients to the bowl and stir to mix.

For the tomato water sauce: Measure the tomato liquid; if necessary, add enough of the tomato juice, Bloody Mary mix, or V8 juice to bring the liquid to 5 tablespoons. Combine the tomato mixture and the remaining ingredients in a bowl, whisking to emulsify the sauce.

At serving time, divide the sauce among four plates. Place a ½-cup ring mold (or an empty tuna fish can with both ends removed) in the center of one of the plates and spoon one quarter of the tomato tartare into the mold. Carefully remove the mold and repeat this procedure on each of the three remaining plates. Sprinkle with the chopped tarragon or chives, decorate with the chive flowers, if desired, and serve.

Tomato tartare

- 1 large tomato (about 12 ounces)
- 2 tablespoons finely chopped sweet onion, such as Vidalia
- ½ cup diced (½-inch) day-old bread (preferably from a country loaf)
- 3 tablespoons good olive oil
- ½ teaspoon salt
- ¼ teaspoon freshly ground black pepper

Tomato water sauce

- Tomato juice, Bloody Mary mix, or V8 juice, if needed
- 5 tablespoons good olive oil
- ½ teaspoon salt
- ¼ teaspoon freshly ground black pepper
- 1 tablespoon finely chopped fresh tarragon or chives
- 2 chive flowers, for garnish (optional)

Multipurpose herbed crumbs

I usually put these out on the table when I serve salads. They add a welcome crunch. They also make a great addition to pasta, soup, gratins, or fish. Chewy country bread makes much better crumbs than ordinary white bread. Depending on how thickly the diced bread is spread on the cookie sheet, it will take from 8 to 15 minutes to brown sufficiently and will shrink as it cooks. Light-textured bread will brown much faster than heavy, tight-textured country bread. ❧ *about 3 cups*

8 ounces country bread with crusts
2 tablespoons good olive oil
1 teaspoon dried thyme leaves
1 teaspoon fresh rosemary leaves, coarsely chopped
¼ teaspoon salt
¼ teaspoon freshly ground black pepper

Heat the oven to 400 degrees. Cut the bread, crusts and all, into ½-inch dice. (You should have about 5 cups.) Scatter the diced bread in a roasting pan, then add the oil, thyme, rosemary, salt, and pepper. Toss to coat the bread thoroughly with the oil and seasonings. Bake for 8 to 15 minutes, or until browned.

Cool to room temperature, then transfer the bread cubes to a plastic bag. Seal the bag, and press on it with your hands or a rolling pin to crush the cubes into coarse crumbs.

◄← MAKE AHEAD
The crumbs will keep in a sealed bag in the refrigerator for up to 2 weeks.

Vegetables

Asparagus with croutons and chorizo

This recipe is inspired by Spanish ingredients and combines them in a quick and tasty way. Spanish chorizo or chouriço, the Portuguese version of this spicy sausage, works well in this recipe. You can also use one of the hotter domestic chorizo sausages—some of which are better than others—available at any supermarket. I prefer to make the croutons with chewy bread.

Depending on the size of the asparagus (I like fat, firm specimens), the cooking time may need to be adjusted by a minute or so. I like my asparagus a bit firm to the bite but not "raw crunchy."   ❧ *4 servings*

Cut each asparagus stalk into 3 or 4 pieces.

At serving time, heat the olive oil in a large skillet over high heat until very hot. Add the asparagus, chorizo, bread, and almonds and sauté, covered, for 5 to 6 minutes, tossing or stirring the mixture a few times, so it browns and cooks all over. Add the salt and pepper, toss again, and serve on four warmed plates.

1 pound large, thick, firm asparagus, tough ends removed and bottom half of stalks peeled with a vegetable peeler

¼ cup good olive oil

1 cup ¾-inch pieces chorizo sausages (about 4 ounces)

1½ cups ¾-inch bread cubes (croutons), preferably from a baguette or country loaf

¼ cup whole almonds with skins

¼ teaspoon salt

¼ teaspoon freshly ground black pepper

About asparagus

You can peel the bottom half of the asparagus stalks to within 3 or 4 inches of the tips as soon as you buy them. A good vegetable peeler makes the job easy. After they are peeled, wrap them in wet paper towels and store in a plastic bag in the refrigerator.

Asparagus custards

At our house, this dish signals the arrival of spring. Make sure you choose asparagus with fat stalks and tight tips, indicating young and fresh specimens. *4 servings*

Bring 2 cups water to a boil in an ovenproof skillet. Add the asparagus, bring the water back to a boil, and cook over high heat, covered, for 2 to 3 minutes, until the asparagus is tender but still firm when pierced with the point of a sharp knife. Drain and place the asparagus on a cutting board. Set the skillet aside.

Cut off the top 3 inches of the asparagus stalks and set these tips aside for garnishing. Cut the remaining stalks into 1-inch pieces and put them in a food processor with the garlic. Process for 10 to 15 seconds, until pureed. Add the eggs, cream, most of the salt (the rest is for the tips), and pepper. Process for 10 seconds.

Heat the oven to 350 degrees. Using about ½ tablespoon of the butter, butter four small custard cups, soufflé molds, or ovenproof glass dishes, each with a capacity of about ½ cup. Divide the asparagus mixture among the molds and arrange them in the reserved skillet with enough tepid tap water to come halfway up the sides of the cups.

Put the skillet in the oven and bake for 25 to 30 minutes, until the custards are set and the point of a knife inserted into the centers comes out clean. Remove the cups from the water bath and let rest for 10 minutes before unmolding.

Split the reserved asparagus tips lengthwise, put them in a skillet or an ovenproof microwavable bowl, and add the remaining dash of salt and the remaining 1½ tablespoons butter. Heat gently in the skillet on top of the stove, or in the bowl in the regular oven or microwave oven, until hot.

At serving time, unmold the custards onto four individual plates and arrange the asparagus tips on top. Serve immediately.

1 pound asparagus, tough ends removed and bottom half of stalks peeled with a vegetable peeler

1 garlic clove, peeled and crushed

3 large eggs

½ cup heavy cream

½ teaspoon salt

¼ teaspoon freshly ground black pepper

2 tablespoons unsalted butter, at room temperature

◂◂ MAKE AHEAD

The custards can be baked a day ahead, then cooled, covered, and refrigerated. Return the custards to the skillet, add water to the skillet, and heat on top of the stove, without letting the water come to a boil, for 10 minutes, or until the custards are hot in the centers.

Broccoli rabe and pea fricassee

For years, I've cooked broccoli rabe like this, with garlic and red pepper. Here, I use large, mild, flavorful elephant garlic, cutting it into flakes with a vegetable peeler. Frozen baby peas are a wonderful complement to seasoned broccoli rabe, giving a hint of sweetness that balances the slight bitterness of the greens. This fricassee goes well with poultry as well as meat. ⚜ *4 servings*

1¼ pounds broccoli rabe (about 10 cups lightly packed)

¼ cup good olive oil

1 large elephant garlic clove, cut with a vegetable peeler into flakes or thin slices (about ⅓ cup)

½ teaspoon crushed red pepper

1 (10-ounce) package frozen baby peas

½ teaspoon salt

Cut off the bottom 4 inches from the stems of the broccoli rabe. Peel them to remove the tough, fibrous outer layer: Using a small paring knife, grab the skin at the end of one stem and pull; it will come off easily. Go around each stem in this manner, removing the fibrous exterior. Cut the broccoli rabe into 2½-inch pieces, wash, and drain in a colander.

Heat the olive oil in a large skillet over high heat. When it is hot, sauté the garlic and crushed red pepper in the oil for 30 seconds. Add about one third of the broccoli, still wet from washing, and stir so that the garlic flakes come to the top of the mixture instead of burning underneath it. Add the remaining broccoli, cover, and cook over high heat for about 5 minutes, or until the broccoli is tender. Add the peas and salt, and cook, uncovered, for 5 minutes longer, or until most of the moisture is gone and the peas are hot.

Serve immediately, or cool, cover, refrigerate, and reheat in a microwave oven at serving time.

Broad beans with shallots

This simple sauté is a good side dish with chicken or veal. Broad beans are available in late summer in my market. Choose young broad beans that are meaty, tender, and flavorful. As they get older, the beans grow inside the pods and the pods toughen and become stringy. Eventually, only the beans inside are edible.

If you can't find broad beans, substitute green or wax beans.

⮑ *6 servings*

1½ pounds fresh broad beans

1 teaspoon salt

2 tablespoons good olive oil

4–5 shallots, cut into thin slices (¾ cup)

½ teaspoon freshly ground black pepper

Remove any strings from the beans, and wash them under cool running water. Drain the beans in a colander.

Pour 2½ cups water into a saucepan and add ½ teaspoon of the salt. Bring the water to a rapid boil. Add the beans, cover, and return to a boil. Cook the beans, covered, over high heat for 9 to 10 minutes, until they are tender but still a bit firm to the bite. Drain the beans, refresh them under cold water, and set aside.

Heat the oil in a skillet over medium heat and add the shallots. Sauté the shallots for about 1 minute, until they are soft and lightly browned. Add the beans, the remaining ½ teaspoon salt, and the pepper, and continue cooking for 3 to 4 minutes longer, or until the vegetables are hot and tender. Serve immediately.

Cauliflower with scallions and sesame oil

Cauliflower appears frequently on my table. This is a quick, warm salad with Asian flavors. Use very white cauliflower for this recipe; darkish spots indicate an older specimen, which tends to be much stronger in taste.   *4 servings*

1 firm, white cauliflower head (about 1½ pounds), trimmed of any green leaves
¼ teaspoon salt
¼ teaspoon freshly ground black pepper
1 tablespoon peanut oil
2 teaspoons dark (Asian) sesame oil
⅓ cup finely minced scallions

Divide the cauliflower into 12 to 14 florets. Bring about ½ inch water to a boil in a stainless steel saucepan and add the florets. Cover and cook over high heat for 8 to 10 minutes, until the cauliflower is tender but still firm. There should be almost no water remaining in the pan.

Transfer the florets to a serving bowl and immediately add the remaining ingredients. Toss gently to coat the cauliflower and serve immediately.

Asparagus with shallots

Sautéing asparagus is a less conventional method of cooking it than steaming or poaching. ❧ *4 servings*

Cut the asparagus stalks on the bias into 2-inch pieces.

Heat the oil in a large skillet or saucepan over medium heat. Add the asparagus and shallots and cook for 7 to 8 minutes, until the asparagus is just tender. Stir in the butter, salt, and pepper and toss to mix. Serve immediately.

1 pound asparagus, tough ends removed and bottom half of stalks peeled with a vegetable peeler

1 tablespoon good olive oil

4–5 shallots, cut into thin slices (¾ cup)

1 tablespoon unsalted butter

½ teaspoon salt

¼ teaspoon freshly ground black pepper

Broccoli puree with brown butter

For this recipe, I puree cooked broccoli florets and flavor the puree with garlic and *beurre noisette*, or nut-brown butter. Reserve about ¾ pound of the stems for Broccoli Stem Relish (page 92).

4 servings

3 bunches broccoli (about 1¾ pounds)

2 garlic cloves, peeled

3 tablespoons unsalted butter

¾ teaspoon salt

¼ teaspoon freshly ground black pepper

Cut the broccoli florets from the stems. (You should have about 1 pound florets.) Reserve the stems (about ¾ pound) for the Broccoli Stem Relish.

Bring about 2 cups water to a boil in a medium saucepan. Add the broccoli florets and the garlic. Bring back to a boil, reduce the heat to low, cover, and cook until tender, about 10 minutes. Drain; reserve the liquid. Put the solids in a food processor.

Melt the butter in a skillet and continue cooking it over medium heat until it turns light brown. Add to the food processor along with the salt, pepper, and 3 tablespoons of the reserved cooking liquid. Process into a fine puree. (You will have about 2 cups.)

Serve immediately, or cool, cover, refrigerate, and reheat in a microwave oven at serving time.

Broccoli stem relish

This spicy, crunchy dish is a great way to use broccoli stems, which I consider to be the best part of that vegetable. You can also make this with cauliflower. Vary the amount of jalapeño and hot chili oil based on your tolerance for hot seasonings. ⤴ *4 servings*

Peel the fibrous exterior of the broccoli stems with a small paring knife. (You should have about 8 ounces peeled broccoli.) Cut the stems into sticks about 2½ inches long and ½ inch thick. (You should have about 2½ cups.)

Put the broccoli sticks in a bowl and toss them with the salt. Let stand at room temperature for at least 30 minutes or up to 1 hour. Drain well, add the remaining ingredients, and mix well before serving.

¾ pound broccoli stems
1 teaspoon salt
1 teaspoon chopped garlic
1 teaspoon Asian-style hot chili oil
1 teaspoon sugar
1 teaspoon balsamic vinegar
1 teaspoon dark (Asian) sesame oil
½ teaspoon finely chopped jalapeño pepper
1 tablespoon finely minced fresh mint

Silky chestnut and apple puree

Whole cooked chestnuts, usually available in jars at supermarkets, are an excellent addition to stuffings and are good served whole as a garnish for roasts. But you'll be surprised what a wonderful puree they make. Serve this with Veal Roast (page 160), lamb, or chicken.   *4 servings*

Put all the ingredients except the butter in a saucepan. Bring to a boil over high heat, then reduce the heat, cover, and cook for 20 minutes. Remove the lid and cook for 6 to 8 minutes longer to reduce the juices. There should be only about ¼ cup liquid remaining.

Transfer the contents of the pan to a food processor, process briefly, then add the butter and process until very smooth. Serve immediately, or cool, refrigerate, and reheat in a microwave oven at serving time.

1 (7.4-ounce) jar roasted whole chestnuts (1½ cups)

1 medium apple (6 ounces), peeled, cored, and cut into 1-inch pieces

¼ cup coarsely chopped onion

1 cup chicken stock, homemade (see page 55), or low-salt canned chicken broth

About ¼ teaspoon salt (less if using canned chicken broth)

¼ teaspoon freshly ground black pepper

1½ tablespoons unsalted butter

About chestnuts

If you want to use fresh chestnuts in this or other savory recipes, score them, roast on a cookie sheet in a 400-degree oven for 10 to 12 minutes until the skins burst open a little, then peel off the outside shells and inside skins and cook in chicken stock or water until tender. When using fresh chestnuts in desserts, after roasting, cook them in water or milk with sugar and a dash of vanilla until tender, then puree.

Chickpea ragout

A versatile dish, this is good as an accompaniment to fish, poultry, and meat, and it can also be served as a first course or, with a couple of fried eggs, as a light main course. It's great poured over pasta, and with the addition of a sausage such as kielbasa, it makes a whole meal. You can also substitute canned red or white beans for the chickpeas.

4 servings

2 tablespoons good olive oil

½ cup diced (½-inch) onion

½ cup chopped scallions

2 cups diced (1-inch) tomatoes

1 tablespoon coarsely chopped garlic

1 (16-ounce) can chickpeas, drained

½ cup chicken stock, homemade (see page 55), or low-salt canned chicken broth

About ½ teaspoon salt (less if using canned chicken broth)

½ teaspoon freshly ground black pepper

1 tablespoon chopped fresh flat-leaf parsley

Heat the oil in a saucepan over high heat and add the onion and scallions. Sauté for 2 to 3 minutes to soften the vegetables, then add the remaining ingredients, except the parsley. Return to a boil, reduce the heat to low, cover, and boil gently for 15 minutes. Remove the lid and boil for a few minutes longer to reduce the liquid.

Divide among four bowls, sprinkle the parsley on top, and serve.

Skillet endives

The classic way of cooking endives is to boil them until tender in a mixture of water, lemon juice, salt, and sugar, then sauté them in a skillet until lightly browned. My method is easier and gives the endives a more concentrated taste.　　　　　＊ *4 servings*

Melt the butter in a nonstick skillet and add the oil. Wash the endives and add them whole and still wet to the skillet. Sprinkle with the salt and sugar, cover, and cook over low heat, turning occasionally, for about 30 minutes, or until the endives are very tender and nicely caramelized all over.

Remove the lid and cook over high heat to evaporate any extra liquid. Serve with the juices and a sprinkling of parsley.

1 tablespoon unsalted butter

1 tablespoon good olive oil

4 large endives (about 1½ pounds total)

½ teaspoon salt

½ teaspoon sugar

1 tablespoon chopped fresh flat-leaf parsley

Creamy lima bean gratin

This easy-to-make gratin is a great accompaniment to roasted lamb or poultry. Other canned beans can be substituted for the limas. ✌ *4 servings*

Put all the ingredients except the butter and cheese in a food processor. Process for 15 to 20 seconds, until very smooth.

Use the butter to coat a small gratin or baking dish with a 2- to 3-cup capacity. Pour the bean mixture into the dish and sprinkle the cheese on top.

When ready to cook the dish, heat the oven to 350 degrees. Bake the gratin for 20 to 30 minutes, until it is nicely browned on top and set. Serve.

1 (8½-ounce) can lima beans, drained

2 large eggs

1 garlic clove, peeled and crushed

½ cup heavy cream

¼ teaspoon salt

¼ teaspoon freshly ground black pepper

1 tablespoon unsalted butter, at room temperature

2 tablespoons grated Swiss (Gruyère or Emmenthaler) cheese

◄← MAKE AHEAD

The dish can be assembled a few hours ahead, then cooked when needed.

Puree of peas with mint and cilantro

Mint, cilantro, and jalapeño give this puree a complex taste. For this recipe, it's essential to use baby peas. Process them immediately after they are cooked and drained. If you allow them to sit unprocessed for even 10 minutes, their skins will shrink and dry out and they can't be pureed properly in the food processor. ❧ *4 servings*

1 pound frozen baby peas
½ cup (loosely packed) fresh mint leaves
½ cup (loosely packed) fresh cilantro leaves
About 2 teaspoons chopped jalapeño pepper (more or less, depending on your tolerance)
½ teaspoon salt
1 teaspoon sugar
1 tablespoon unsalted butter
1 tablespoon good olive oil

Bring 3 cups salted water to a boil. Add the frozen peas and return to a boil, which will take 3 to 4 minutes. Boil gently for 1½ minutes, then drain in a colander, reserving a few spoonfuls of the cooking liquid.

Immediately transfer the peas to a food processor and add the remaining ingredients and up to 2 tablespoons of the reserved cooking liquid, if the mixture is too thick to puree properly. Process to a fine puree.

Serve immediately, or if the puree is made ahead, reheat in a microwave oven before serving. (You will have 1⅔ cups.)

About peas

Frozen baby peas are also sold labeled "tender" or "petite." These names denote the very smallest peas from each pod, which are sweeter and tenderer than the large, starchy ones from which they are separated.

Sautéed plantains

I've eaten sautéed plantains many times in restaurants and homes, but they are never as good as those prepared from my wife's recipe, which she got from her Puerto Rican mother. The big difference is that Grandma left her plantains at room temperature for several days or even weeks, until they turned completely—and I do mean *completely*—black, when most people would have thought they were spoiled. As a result of this long ripening, they became sweeter, softer, and more flavorful than yellow-brown plantains, which tend to end up dry, mealy, and bland when sautéed.

2 black-skinned plantains (1 pound total), also called "cooking bananas"

1 tablespoon unsalted butter

½ teaspoon canola oil

4 servings

If not serving the sautéed plantains immediately, heat the oven to 180 degrees.

Cut off both ends of each plantain and slit the skin lengthwise with a sharp knife. Peel off the skin carefully, so that you don't damage the flesh, and cut each plantain in half lengthwise.

Heat a nonstick skillet over medium to high heat, and add the butter and oil. Add the plantain pieces cut sides up and cook them gently for about 2½ minutes. Turn them over and cook for 2 minutes. The plantains should be nicely browned on both sides.

Using a small skillet, meat pounder, or metal measuring cup, press gently but firmly on each plantain half to crush it slightly. Reduce the heat to very low, turn the plantains again, and continue cooking for about 2 minutes longer, or until they are soft and dark brown. Serve immediately or keep warm in the oven until ready to eat.

Crusty tomato savory

This tasty tomato gratin is a great accompaniment to eggs —poached, fried, or omelets—and is good with poached or steamed fish or shellfish. ❧ *4 servings*

2 pounds ripe plum tomatoes

3 slices white bread (about 2½ ounces)

⅓ cup coarsely chopped fresh chives

2 teaspoons coarsely chopped fresh thyme leaves

1 tablespoon good olive oil

2 tablespoons unsalted butter

½ teaspoon salt

½ teaspoon freshly ground black pepper

Submerge the tomatoes in a large saucepan of boiling water for 30 to 45 seconds, then drain. When they are cool enough to handle, peel them and discard the skins. Halve the tomatoes horizontally, press out the seeds, and cut the flesh into 1-inch pieces.

Heat the oven to 425 degrees. Arrange the bread slices on a cookie sheet and bake for 5 to 7 minutes, until nicely browned on both sides. (There is no need to turn the bread; it will brown on both sides.) When cool enough to handle, cut or break the slices into ½-inch pieces. Put the bread pieces in a blender with the chives and thyme and blend for 30 to 45 seconds, until smooth and well blended. Add the oil and blend for 5 seconds.

Melt the butter in a saucepan and cook it over medium to high heat until browned to a hazelnut color. Add the tomato pieces, salt, and pepper. Cook over high heat for 2 to 3 minutes, or until the mixture is hot and has a relatively soft consistency.

Heat the broiler. Pour the tomatoes into a gratin dish or baking dish large enough so that the tomatoes are about ¾ inch thick in the dish. Top with the crumb mixture and broil about 5 inches from the heat source for 5 to 7 minutes, or until the crumb topping is nicely browned and crusty. Serve immediately.

⤙ MAKE AHEAD

You can set the tomatoes aside in the gratin dish for a while. Reheat them in a microwave oven before adding the crumb topping and finish the dish under the broiler. Serve immediately.

Mushroom and raisin chutney

Serve this dish as an hors d'oeuvre, part of antipasti, or as a chutney with pâtés or cold roasted pork, chicken, or turkey. You can make it with white button mushrooms, as I do here, or with wild mushrooms available at the supermarket.

❧ 4 servings

Put all the ingredients in a nonreactive (stainless steel) saucepan. Bring to a boil, cover, reduce the heat to low, and boil gently for 5 minutes. Cool.

Serve cold from the refrigerator or at room temperature.

❧ **MAKE AHEAD**
   The chutney will keep for a couple of weeks in the refrigerator.

1 pound white button mushrooms, quartered (about 5 cups)

⅓ cup dark raisins

2 tablespoons good olive oil

2 tablespoons tomato paste

½ teaspoon mustard seeds

2 bay leaves

⅓ cup dry white wine

1 tablespoon chopped garlic

2 teaspoons chopped peeled fresh ginger

½ cup coarsely chopped onion

3 tablespoons red wine vinegar

1½ teaspoons sugar

½ teaspoon freshly ground black pepper

1 teaspoon salt

Rice, potatoes, and pasta

Soupy rice with peas

This is my interpretation of *arroz asopao*, "soupy" rice in the Puerto Rican style. A special celebration of spring, this recipe incorporates fresh peas, although it can be made with frozen peas or fresh asparagus.

The dish takes about 30 minutes to prepare from start to finish and should be served immediately. We like it as a main course for a light dinner, when we eat it from soup bowls with soupspoons. Half of this recipe makes a great first course or is an excellent accompaniment to roasted veal or chicken.

❧ 4 servings

3 tablespoons good olive oil

1 cup chopped onion

2 teaspoons chopped garlic

1½ cups Arborio rice

About ½ teaspoon salt (less if using canned chicken broth)

¼ teaspoon freshly ground black pepper

5 cups chicken stock, homemade (see page 55), or low-salt canned chicken broth

1 pound fresh peas, shelled, or 1¼ cups frozen baby peas, or 1¼ pounds asparagus, tough ends removed, bottom half of stalks peeled with a vegetable peeler, and stalks cut into 1-inch pieces

2 tablespoons unsalted butter

½ cup freshly grated Parmesan cheese

1 tablespoon chopped fresh chives (optional)

Heat the oil in a heavy saucepan over medium heat and add the onion and garlic. Cook gently for 2 to 3 minutes, or until slightly softened. Add the rice, stir well, then add the salt and pepper. Add 3 cups of the stock, cover, reduce the heat to low, and cook for about 8 minutes. Stir well to prevent the mixture from sticking on the bottom.

Add 1 cup of the stock and cook for 6 minutes, uncovered, stirring occasionally, over medium heat. Add ½ cup of the stock, and continue cooking, uncovered, for 6 minutes, stirring occasionally.

Add the remaining ½ cup stock and the peas or asparagus pieces and cook gently over medium heat, scraping the bottom of the pan with a wooden spatula every couple of minutes, for 8 to 10 minutes longer, for a total of about 30 minutes. The rice should be soft and soupy, tender but still firm to the bite.

Gently stir in the butter and Parmesan cheese. Divide among four warmed soup plates, sprinkle with chives if you like, and serve immediately.

Couscous

I usually serve this with Pressure-Cooker Lamb and White Bean Stew (page 170), but it's delicious with most stews or even fish.   ❦ *4 servings*

1   cup water
¼   teaspoon salt
1¼ cups quick-cooking couscous (12 ounces)
1½ tablespoons good olive oil

Pour the water into a large glass measuring cup or any other microwavable container and add the salt. Place in a microwave oven and heat for 2 to 3 minutes, or until the water starts to boil.

Remove the water from the microwave, add the couscous and oil, and mix lightly with a spoon. Cover tightly with plastic wrap and set aside for 5 minutes. Then, using a fork, stir to separate the grains. Serve.

⊰ MAKE AHEAD

The couscous can be prepared about 1 hour ahead. Cover with plastic wrap and reheat in the microwave oven for about 1½ minutes, just until warm.

Baked potatoes with chive sour cream

My family loves baked potatoes, but they take a good hour to cook properly in a conventional oven. Recently Gloria worked out a recipe using a microwave oven in conjunction with a regular oven. ❧ *4 servings*

4 large baking potatoes (each about 12 ounces), as blemish free as possible

1 cup sour cream

¼ cup finely minced fresh chives

½ teaspoon salt

½ teaspoon freshly ground black pepper

Heat the oven to 450 degrees. Scrub the potatoes with a vegetable brush under running water, then use a paring knife to scrape off any dark spots not removed by the brush. Put the potatoes in a microwave oven and cook them at 100-percent power for 4 minutes. Turn them over and cook in the microwave for 4 minutes longer. The potatoes should be cooked or almost cooked at this point.

Transfer the potatoes to the oven and bake for 12 to 15 minutes, until they are soft inside with crisp skin.

Meanwhile, combine the sour cream, chives, salt, and pepper in a small bowl.

Without cutting completely through the potatoes, make a lengthwise and a crosswise cut on the top of each. Then, using your index fingers and thumbs, grasp the potatoes and press on all four sides of each to open them in the center. Serve with the chives and sour cream.

Cubed potatoes with garlic and sage

This homey, assertively flavored potato and garlic dish goes well with poultry and grilled or roasted meat. Though left whole, the garlic cloves are quite mild when cooked this way. If fresh sage is not available, substitute fresh thyme, savory, oregano, chives, or basil.　　✌ *4 servings*

1¾	pounds baking potatoes, peeled and cut into 1-inch cubes (about 4 cups)
1	tablespoon unsalted butter
2	tablespoons corn oil
24	medium garlic cloves, peeled
¼	teaspoon salt
⅛	teaspoon freshly ground black pepper
1½	tablespoons shredded fresh sage leaves

Rinse the potato cubes in cool water and drain them well.

Heat the butter and oil in a skillet (preferably nonstick) until hot but not smoking. Add the potatoes, cover, and cook them over medium heat for 10 minutes, turning occasionally, or until they are nicely browned. Add the garlic and cook, covered, for 10 minutes longer over low heat.

Add the salt, pepper, and sage and toss to mix. Serve immediately.

Summertime pasta

This simple pasta dish of shells, combined with a vegetable salad, is a hot-weather staple at our house.

Warm the vegetable salad in a microwave oven for a few minutes to soften it slightly before tossing it with the hot pasta. Be sure to serve the pasta on warmed plates, preferably soup plates. ☙ *4 servings*

Mix the tomatoes, zucchini, mushrooms, salt, pepper, and olive oil in a large microwavable glass bowl.

About 20 minutes before serving time, bring 2 quarts salted water to a boil in a large saucepan or pot. Add the pasta, stir well, and return to a boil. Boil, uncovered, over high heat until cooked to your liking (slightly al dente for me).

Meanwhile, put the bowl containing the vegetables in a microwave oven and cook on high for 2 minutes, or until lukewarm.

Drain the pasta thoroughly and add it to the warmed vegetable salad. Sprinkle with the cheese and basil and toss well. Divide among four warmed soup plates. Serve immediately.

Variation

To make a bread salad, combine the tomatoes, zucchini, mushrooms, oil, and basil, and add 2 to 3 cups 1-inch pieces of bread (preferably from a chewy baguette or country loaf). Let the bread soak up the oil and vegetable juices for about 30 minutes, add salt and pepper to taste, and serve.

3 cups diced (1-inch) ripe tomatoes (about 1 pound total)

1½ cups diced (½-inch) zucchini (1 zucchini; about 6 ounces)

1 cup diced (½-inch) white button mushrooms

1 teaspoon salt

¾ teaspoon freshly ground black pepper

⅓ cup extra-virgin olive oil

6 ounces pasta shells

1 cup freshly grated Parmesan cheese

1½ cups (loosely packed) coarsely shredded fresh basil

Wonton cannelloni in tomato sauce

One day while I was shredding wonton skins to use in place of noodles in a Chinese soup, I decided to make cannelloni with them. They don't have to be precooked like dried pasta, and I like the taste and texture of the wonton skins.

≈ 4 servings

Heat the oven to 375 degrees. Put the tomatoes with their liquid, garlic, ¾ teaspoon of the salt, half of the pepper, the olive oil, and the Italian seasoning in a food processor and process until smooth.

Mix the ricotta, eggs, remaining salt and pepper, and 2 tablespoons of the chives in a bowl.

Pour ½ cup of the tomato sauce into a rectangular baking dish (about 11 by 9 inches). Place a wonton skin on top of the sauce in the dish and spoon about ⅓ cup of the ricotta mixture into the middle of the skin. Bring two opposite sides of the wonton skin over the cheese filling to enclose it, creating a roll. Repeat with the 5 remaining wonton skins, arranging the filled cannelloni in the baking dish seam sides down as you go along so that they are lined up in a row next to one another in the dish.

Pour the remaining sauce over the cannelloni (it will fill the spaces between the cannelloni and even out the surface). Place the baking dish on a cookie sheet, sprinkle the mozzarella and Parmesan cheeses on top, and bake for 15 minutes.

Sprinkle the cannelloni with the remaining 2 tablespoons chives and serve immediately.

1 (28-ounce) can Italian-style tomatoes
3 garlic cloves
1½ teaspoons salt
¾ teaspoon freshly ground black pepper
2 tablespoons good olive oil
1 teaspoon Italian seasoning
1 pound ricotta cheese
2 large eggs
4 tablespoons chopped fresh chives
6 wonton skins, each 6 inches square (¾ ounce)
1 cup grated mozzarella cheese (about 7 ounces)
2 tablespoons freshly grated Parmesan cheese

◄← MAKE AHEAD
The gratin can be kept in a 180-degree oven for up to 45 minutes before serving.

Pasta, ham, and vegetable gratin

My mother loved gratins, and leftover meat and cold cuts always found their way into our pasta, usually along with zucchini or peas. I have made gratins for my family through the years.

❧ *4 servings*

Bring about 2 quarts salted water to a boil in a large saucepan. Add the pasta, stir well, and return to a boil. Boil, uncovered, until cooked but still slightly firm, or al dente, about 12 minutes. Drain, cool under cold running water, then drain again. (You will have about 3 cups.)

Put the cooked pasta in a large bowl and stir in the ham, corn, peas, zucchini, salt, pepper, and Swiss cheese.

For the white sauce: Melt the butter in a saucepan, add the flour, and mix it in with a whisk. Add the milk and bring to a boil, stirring occasionally with the whisk, especially at the edges of the saucepan. The sauce should thicken. Remove the pan from the heat, and mix in the cream. Let cool to lukewarm.

Heat the broiler. Combine the sauce with the pasta mixture in the bowl and transfer to a gratin dish or shallow baking dish with about a 6-cup capacity. Sprinkle the Parmesan cheese on top.

Broil about 4 inches from the heat source for 6 to 8 minutes, or until bubbly hot and the surface is lightly browned. Serve immediately.

About 1¾ cups pasta shells or penne (about 5 ounces)

1½ cups diced (½-inch) cooked ham (about 7 ounces)

¾ cup corn kernels (from about 1 ear corn)

½ cup peas, fresh or frozen

1½ cups cubed (½-inch) zucchini

¾ teaspoon salt

¾ teaspoon freshly ground black pepper

¾ cup grated Swiss (Gruyère or Emmenthaler) cheese

White sauce

2 tablespoons unsalted butter

2 tablespoons all-purpose flour

2 cups milk

½ cup heavy cream

2 tablespoons freshly grated Parmesan cheese

◄← MAKE AHEAD

The gratin can be made ahead, sprinkled with Parmesan, and kept, covered, at room temperature for a few hours or refrigerated for up to a day before it is finished in the oven. If refrigerated, bring back to room temperature and bake on a cookie sheet for about 30 minutes in a 425-degree oven until heated through and lightly browned on top. Do not try to keep the cooked gratin in a warm oven for more than 10 to 15 minutes, or the pasta will swell up in the liquid and become gooey.

Fish and shellfish

Halibut on fresh polenta with pepper oil

A simple poached fish is served on a fresh corn kernel puree that cooks almost instantly. The beautiful red pepper oil topping is made from a bell pepper liquefied in a blender with a little olive oil.

Striped bass, swordfish, or even salmon can be used instead of halibut. ❧ *4 servings*

Put the red pepper pieces in a blender with ¼ teaspoon of the salt and the olive oil and process until smooth. Transfer to a microwavable bowl.

Bring about 1½ quarts salted water to a boil in a large skillet.

Meanwhile, put the corn kernels in a blender and process until smooth. (You will have about 2 cups.)

Heat the butter in a saucepan, and add the corn puree along with the remaining ½ teaspoon salt and the pepper. Bring to a boil and cook for about 30 seconds, or until the puree thickens. Set aside while you poach the fish.

Drop the halibut steaks into the boiling water. Reduce the heat to low and cook the fish at a low boil for 2 to 3 minutes, depending on the thickness of the fish and your own taste preferences.

Meanwhile, heat the pepper oil in a microwave oven for 1 minute. Divide the corn puree among four plates. Lift the fish out of the water with a skimmer or fish spatula, pat it dry with paper towels, and place a steak on top of the polenta on each plate. Spoon on the hot pepper oil, sprinkle on the chives, and serve immediately.

1 red bell pepper, skin removed with a vegetable peeler, seeded, and flesh cut into 1-inch pieces (about 1 cup)

¾ teaspoon salt

2 tablespoons extra-virgin olive oil

2½ cups corn kernels (from about 4 ears corn)

2 tablespoons unsalted butter

¼ teaspoon freshly ground black pepper

4 small halibut steaks (each about 4 ounces and ¾ inch thick)

1 tablespoon chopped fresh chives

Grilled striped bass with pimiento relish

Every fall a few friends and I rent a boat and go fishing for striped bass in Long Island Sound. The wild stripers we catch are among the best fish I have ever eaten. Their firm, moist flesh is always a hit with our guests.

In this recipe, I grill the fillets and keep them warm in the oven. At serving time, I add a relish of pimientos and black olives. Feel free to vary the relish ingredients and make use of whatever fresh herbs you have available. Also, if striped bass is not available, use very fresh red snapper, cod, sea bass, or grouper instead.   ❧ *4 servings*

For the striped bass: Heat the oven to 180 degrees. Heat a grill until very hot. (I like to use a nonstick grill pan when not cooking outdoors.) Rub the steaks with the oil and sprinkle them with the salt and pepper. Arrange the steaks on the hot grill and cook them for about 1½ minutes on each side so that they are nicely grill-marked on both sides. Transfer the steaks to an ovenproof platter and keep them warm in the oven until ready to serve.

Meanwhile, make the relish: Mix the pimiento strips, olives, scallions, lemon juice, and olive oil in a small bowl. Arrange a fish fillet on each of four warmed plates. Top with the relish and serve.

Striped bass

- 4 striped bass fillet steaks (each about 6 ounces and 1 inch thick)
- 2 teaspoons canola oil
- ½ teaspoon salt
- ½ teaspoon freshly ground black pepper

Pimiento relish

- ½ cup canned or jarred red pimientos, cut into thin julienne strips
- About 24 oil-cured black olives, pitted
- ¼ cup finely minced scallions
- 2 tablespoons fresh lemon juice
- 3 tablespoons extra-virgin olive oil

❧ **MAKE AHEAD**
The fish can be grilled and kept warm in a low oven for up to 30 minutes before serving.

Oven-baked salmon with sun-dried tomato and salsa mayonnaise

This dish is the essence of my fast food. Season a fillet of salmon and nutty bread crumbs right on your serving platter and bake it in a very low oven while you make another dish or entertain your guests. Don't worry about burning the platter; it won't be damaged by the low heat of the oven, and the fish will be perfectly cooked. ❧ *About 12 servings*

Heat the oven to 200 degrees. Oil a platter with the oil. Arrange the salmon on the platter and sprinkle it with ¾ teaspoon salt and ½ teaspoon pepper. Turn the salmon over and sprinkle it with the remaining ¾ teaspoon salt and ½ teaspoon pepper. Sprinkle the hazelnut-crumb mixture on top of the fillet. Bake for 40 to 45 minutes, until the salmon is barely cooked. (I like it slightly rare inside.)

Meanwhile, for the mayonnaise: Put the sun-dried tomatoes and their oil in a food processor with the salsa. Process until smooth. Transfer to a medium bowl and mix in the salt, mayonnaise, and chives.

When the salmon is done, remove it from the oven and sprinkle the chopped herbs on top. Serve warm or at room temperature with the mayonnaise.

◂◂ MAKE AHEAD

The fish can be made 1 to 2 hours ahead. The mayonnaise can be made up to 1 day ahead and refrigerated.

1 teaspoon canola oil

1 large skinless and boneless salmon fillet (about 3 pounds)

1½ teaspoons salt

1 teaspoon freshly ground black pepper

About 1 cup combined bread crumbs and ground hazelnuts (from 1 slice bread and ¼ cup hazelnuts processed in a food processor)

Salsa mayonnaise

4 ounces sun-dried tomatoes packed in oil (about ¾ cup)

¾ cup Red Hot Salsa (page 41) or fresh store-bought salsa

¼ teaspoon salt

2 cups mayonnaise

3 tablespoons chopped fresh chives

1 cup coarsely chopped fresh herbs (a mixture of parsley, tarragon, chives, and chervil)

Glazed salmon in mirin

The marinade gives the salmon a sweet, nutty flavor and a beautiful color, while the lemon dressing provides a good contrast to the sweetness of the fish. Although I suggest marinating the salmon for at least an hour and as long as overnight, you can just coat the steaks with the marinade and cook them right away, if you are pressed for time.

❧ 4 servings

For the marinade and fish: Combine all the marinade ingredients in a small bowl. Pour the marinade into a plastic zipperlock bag. Put the salmon steaks into the bag, seal the bag, and marinate the steaks in the refrigerator for at least an hour.

For the dressing: When ready to cook the salmon, whisk all the ingredients together in a small bowl until combined and set aside.

Heat a large nonstick skillet until hot. Remove the salmon steaks from the marinade and arrange them in the hot skillet with the marinade on top. Cover and cook over medium to high heat for about 2 minutes, or until the bottoms of the steaks are nicely browned and the tops are cooked through from the steam created in the covered pan. The steaks should be slightly rare in the center.

Serve the salmon steaks with the lemon dressing drizzled over and around them and the sesame seeds sprinkled on top.

Marinade

- 1½ tablespoons mirin (see page 27)
- 1 tablespoon soy sauce
- 1 teaspoon brown sugar
- 1 teaspoon Tabasco sauce

- 4 salmon steaks (each 5–6 ounces and about 1 inch thick)

Lemon dressing

- 2 tablespoons extra-virgin olive oil
- 1 tablespoon fresh lemon juice
- 1 teaspoon dark (Asian) sesame oil
- ¼ teaspoon salt
- ¼ teaspoon Tabasco sauce

- 2 teaspoons sesame seeds, toasted in a nonstick skillet

━━━━━━━━━━━

↤ MAKE AHEAD

For this fast, easy recipe, the salmon can be marinated in the refregerator overnight.

Codfish in walnut-cilantro sauce

This spicy walnut-based sauce goes particularly well with cod, which is a fairly mild fish, but it's also good with poached or baked chicken. If you don't like cilantro, replace it with flat-leaf parsley. Tomato juice can be substituted for the V8 juice.   ✎ *4 servings*

For the sauce: Heat the oven to 400 degrees. Spread the walnuts on a cookie sheet and toast for 7 to 8 minutes, until they are lightly browned. Put the walnuts and the remaining sauce ingredients except the cilantro in a mini-chop or blender and blend until the mixture is creamy and well emulsified. Transfer to a bowl and stir in the cilantro. (You will have 1¼ cups.) Cover and refrigerate the sauce until serving time.

For the cod: About 15 minutes before serving time, heat the oven to 400 degrees. Line a cookie sheet with aluminum foil. Arrange the fish fillets on the lined sheet, spoon the olive oil on top of them, and turn the fillets over so that they are oiled on both sides. Sprinkle the fillets with the salt and roast for about 10 minutes, or until they are just cooked through.

Spoon 2 to 3 tablespoons of the sauce into the center of each of four dinner plates and place a cooked fillet on top of the sauce on each plate. Add another dab of sauce to the top of the fillets and serve immediately.

About cod

Codfish fillets are usually thick on one side and have a thinner tail. Fold the tail underneath so that the fillets are of about equal thickness throughout so they will cook evenly.

Walnut-cilantro sauce

- 1 cup walnut pieces
- ½ teaspoon ground cumin
- 3 garlic cloves
- ¼ teaspoon salt
- 1 small jalapeño pepper, seeded and cut into 1-inch pieces (more or less, depending on your tolerance)
- 1 tablespoon apple cider vinegar
- ½ cup V8 juice
- ½ cup water
- ¼ cup finely chopped fresh cilantro leaves

Cod

- 4 codfish fillets (each about 6 ounces and 1 inch thick)
- 1 tablespoon good olive oil
- ½ teaspoon salt

◄← **MAKE AHEAD**
The sauce will keep for at least 2 weeks in the refrigerator.

Slow-cooked tuna steaks with tomato relish

Here's an excellent example of convenience cooking that produces superb results. Slow-baked tuna steaks are served with a relish of tomato, sweet onion, and hot salsa. This slow-baking technique works with other fish steaks, too, such as halibut.   ❧ *4 servings*

Heat the oven to 200 degrees. Rub the tuna steaks on both sides with the canola oil and sprinkle them with the salt and pepper. Arrange the steaks on a serving plate, or on four dinner plates, and bake for about 20 minutes, for rare. If you want the fish cooked to medium, leave it in for a few more minutes.

Meanwhile, for the tomato relish: Mix the tomato, onion, chives, salt, and salsa in a medium bowl. Add the lime juice and olive oil and mix well.

Remove the tuna steaks from the oven and spoon the sauce liberally over and around the steaks. Serve immediately.

4 center-cut tuna steaks (each about 6 ounces and ¾ inch thick)

1 teaspoon canola oil

¾ teaspoon salt

¾ teaspoon freshly ground black pepper

Tomato relish

¾ cup diced (½-inch) peeled and seeded tomato

½ cup diced (¼-inch) sweet onion, such as Vidalia

3 tablespoons chopped fresh chives

¼ teaspoon salt

⅓ cup Red Hot Salsa (page 41) or fresh store-bought salsa

3 tablespoons fresh lime juice

3 tablespoons good olive oil

Red snapper with mussels and chorizo

I love Spanish food, which is just beginning to be appreciated in the United States. This stew of fish, sausage, and potatoes is a classic combination, earthy and full of flavor. Chorizo (in Spanish) or chouriço (in Portuguese) is a type of kielbasa sausage that is well spiced and lean and contains sizable pieces of meat. I use red snapper here, but black sea bass or even halibut can be substituted.

4 servings

1 pound mussels, well scrubbed (about 24 mussels)
¼ cup dry white wine
¼ cup water
3 tablespoons good olive oil
2 potatoes (about 12 ounces), peeled and each cut into 16 slices (¼ inch thick)
1 piece (5–6 ounces) chorizo sausage, cut into 16 slices (¼ inch thick)
⅓ cup chopped onion
2 teaspoons chopped garlic
½ teaspoon freshly ground black pepper
Salt
4 red snapper fillets (each about 6 ounces)
1 tablespoon chopped fresh parsley

Put the mussels in a stainless steel saucepan with the wine and water and bring to a boil over high heat. Cover and boil for 3 to 4 minutes, until the mussels open, then drain, reserving the liquid. (You should have about 1 cup; add water if necessary.) Discard any mussels that do not open. Remove and discard the top shells from the mussels and set them aside in their half shells in a bowl. When the sediment in the reserved liquid has settled to the bottom, carefully pour the liquid over the mussels in the bowl, leaving the sediment behind and discarding it.

Heat 2 tablespoons of the oil in a large skillet or saucepan over medium heat. When the oil is hot, add the potatoes and chorizo and cook for 8 to 10 minutes, or until both are lightly browned and tender. Add the onion and garlic and cook for 10 seconds, then stir in the reserved mussels and juice. Bring to a boil, reduce the heat, and boil very gently for 2 minutes. Add ¼ teaspoon of the pepper and salt to taste, depending on the saltiness of the mussel liquid.

Meanwhile, heat the broiler. Rub the fish fillets on both sides with the remaining 1 tablespoon of oil and sprinkle them with ¼ teaspoon salt and the remaining ¼ teaspoon pepper. Arrange

the fillets skin sides up on a cookie sheet. Broil 3 to 4 inches from the heat source for 3 to 4 minutes, depending on the thickness of the fillets and how you like your fish.

Ladle some potatoes, chorizo, and mussels into four soup plates with some of the broth. Arrange a fish fillet on top of each serving, sprinkle with the parsley, and serve.

Red snapper with tomatoes and cream

In this festive dish, perfect for a birthday or anniversary, gently poached snapper is served on a bed of tomato and onions and topped with an elegant cream sauce.

Scrod or grouper also works well in this recipe.

4 servings

Put the onions and olive oil in a large skillet with the water. Cook over high heat for about 3 minutes, or until the liquid is gone and the onions are lightly browned. Add the diced tomato, sauté for 1 minute, then set aside and keep warm.

Arrange the fish fillets in one layer in another large skillet and add the wine and ½ teaspoon of the salt. Cover, bring to a boil, then reduce the heat and boil very gently for about 2 minutes, or until the fish is tender but not overcooked. (The timing will depend on the thickness of the fillets.)

Transfer the fish to a platter and set aside in a warm place. Add the cream to the liquid remaining in the skillet used to cook the fish and boil over high heat for a few minutes to reduce it to 1 cup. Add the remaining ½ teaspoon salt, pepper, and dissolved potato starch and mix well.

To serve, divide the warm red onion–tomato mixture among four plates and arrange a piece of fish on top. Coat with the cream sauce, sprinkle with the chives, and serve immediately.

2 cups sliced red onions

2 teaspoons good olive oil

⅓ cup water

1½ cups diced (1-inch) tomato, from 1 large or 2 medium peeled and seeded tomatoes

4 red snapper fillets (each about 6 ounces)

¾ cup dry white wine

1 teaspoon salt

½ cup heavy cream

¼ teaspoon freshly ground black pepper

½ teaspoon potato starch dissolved in 1 tablespoon water

1 tablespoon chopped fresh chives

Poached tilapia with herbed cream sauce

This herb sauce is my mother's classic dressing for young salad greens, particularly Boston lettuce. I've found that it enhances any poached fresh fish, from salmon to trout. The addition of horseradish gives the dressing a special accent. For best results, make it at the last minute.

4 servings

Bring about 1 quart water to a boil in a large skillet and add the salt. Drop the fish fillets into the boiling water and bring the water back to a gentle boil. Cover and remove from the heat. Let stand in the hot water for about 1 minute.

Meanwhile, for the sauce: Pour the cream into a small bowl and add the salt and pepper. Whip with a whisk for about 15 seconds, or just until frothy. Stir in the remaining ingredients.

Using a skimmer, remove the fish from the water and blot dry with paper towels. Place a fillet on each of four warmed plates and coat with the sauce. Serve immediately.

½ teaspoon salt

4 small tilapia fillets (each 3–4 ounces and ½ inch thick)

Herbed cream sauce

½ cup heavy cream

½ teaspoon salt

½ teaspoon freshly ground black pepper

1 tablespoon red wine vinegar

½ tablespoon coarsely chopped fresh tarragon

½ tablespoon coarsely chopped fresh chives

1 tablespoon bottled horseradish

Shrimp and scallop pillows on boston lettuce

These are my variation on Chinese pot stickers. I turn scallops into a mousse in seconds in a food processor and then fold in the shrimp. The pasta for the pillows is pot-sticker rounds, available in packages in many supermarkets and all Asian markets. These pillows are great one per person as a first course or three per person as a main course.

≈ *12 pillows (4 main-course servings)*

Cut the shrimp into 1-inch pieces, setting aside the tail ends (about ¼ cup) as you chop. Put the scallops and shrimp tails in a food processor and process for 15 seconds. Add the sour cream, salt, and pepper and process until smooth. Transfer the mousse to a bowl and fold in the shrimp pieces.

Stack up 3 of the potsticker rounds on the table. Using a rolling pin, press and roll the pile of rounds until they are 4 inches in diameter. (They will not stick to one another or the table.) Repeat with 9 more rounds, rolling 3 at time, so you have 12 rounds that are about 4 inches in diameter.

Arrange the remaining twelve 3-inch rounds side by side on the table. Divide the mousse among them with a spoon or an ice cream scoop, placing about ¼ cup mousse in the center of each. Dampen your finger with water and wet the edges of the 4-inch rounds on one side. Center them wet sides down on top of the mounds of mousse. Press lightly on top and firmly around the edges to seal the rounds together and enclose the mousse. The larger rounds will wrap around the mousse and adhere at the edges to the smaller rounds underneath. Set aside.

At cooking time, arrange about 6 pillows in a nonstick skillet large enough to accommodate them in one layer with no overlap. Pour ¾ cup water and 1 scant tablespoon peanut oil over the pillows and bring to a boil over high heat. Cover, reduce the heat to medium, and cook for about 3 minutes, or until most of the water has evaporated. Remove the lid and cook over medium to high heat for a few minutes, or until all the liquid is gone and the pillows begin to brown in the oil. Continue browning for about 1½ minutes on each side, then transfer to a serving plate. Repeat with the remaining 6 pillows, another ¾ cup water, and the remaining 1 scant tablespoon peanut oil.

½ pound shrimp, shelled

½ pound scallops

⅓ cup sour cream

½ teaspoon salt

¼ teaspoon freshly ground black pepper

24 potsticker rounds (each 3 inches in diameter; also called dumpling, gyoza, or jiaozi wrappers)

2 scant tablespoons peanut oil

Boston lettuce salad

2 tablespoons extra-virgin olive oil

1 teaspoon fresh lemon juice

¼ teaspoon salt

6 cups (loosely packed) torn Boston lettuce leaves, washed and dried (1 large head)

For the salad: In a bowl large enough to hold the lettuce, mix the olive oil, lemon juice, and salt. Add the lettuce and toss to coat the leaves with the dressing.

At serving time, divide the salad among four plates and serve the pillows on top.

Variations

You can fill custard cups with the mousse and bake them in a water bath at 350 degrees for 20 minutes. Alternatively, you can mold the mousse into patties and brown them in a skillet without the pasta, or you can drop tablespoons of the mousse into hot water (just under a boil) and poach them for 5 to 6 minutes. Serve with soup or salad.

Crab cakes in red sauce

When a few guests pop in unexpectedly, try this quick dish made from pasteurized crabmeat and a few pantry ingredients. If you use fresh crabmeat, the crab cakes will be even better and more delicate. *4 servings*

Put the crabmeat in a bowl and add ⅔ cup of the bread crumbs, scallion, cilantro, garlic, mayonnaise, Tabasco, and salt. Mix lightly, just until the ingredients are well combined.

Put the remaining bread crumbs in a food processor with the almonds and process until the nuts are well chopped and combined with the bread.

Heat the oven to 180 degrees. Form the crab mixture into 4 patties, then dip each patty into the crumb mixture until it is coated on all sides.

Heat the oil in a nonstick skillet over medium heat and arrange the patties next to one another in the pan, handling them gently because they are soft. Cook for about 3 minutes on each side. Keep warm in the oven.

Meanwhile, for the sauce: Combine all the ingredients in a bowl.

At serving time, divide the sauce among four plates. Place a patty in the center of the sauce on each plate, sprinkle some chives on the sauce, and serve immediately.

1 (8-ounce) package pasteurized crabmeat or 8 ounces fresh crabmeat, drained and picked clean of shell

1¼ cups fresh bread crumbs (from about 2 slices white bread processed in a food processor)

2 tablespoons minced scallion

2 tablespoons chopped fresh cilantro

1 teaspoon chopped garlic

3 tablespoons mayonnaise

¼ teaspoon Tabasco sauce

¼ teaspoon salt

⅓ cup sliced almonds

2 tablespoons peanut or canola oil

Red sauce

⅓ cup mayonnaise

2 tablespoons ketchup

1 teaspoon wasabi paste (in a tube) or wasabi powder

2 teaspoons fresh lime juice

1 tablespoon water

2 teaspoons chopped fresh chives

Fast lobster fricassee

Boiling isn't the only way to prepare lobster. Cooking lobster in a skillet keeps the meat tender and moist, and the tomato sauce turns it into a flavorful fricassee. Serve this dish to a casual gathering of good friends, and tell them to eat it with their fingers. ❧ *4 servings*

2 lobsters, preferably female (each 1¾–2 pounds)
½ cup dry white wine
⅓ cup good olive oil
¼ teaspoon salt
¼ teaspoon freshly ground black pepper
About ⅓ cup Wondra flour
1 cup chopped onion
⅔ cup chopped scallions
1½ tablespoons chopped garlic
1 cup diced (1-inch) tomato
2 tablespoons chopped fresh flat-leaf parsley

Insert the point of a knife at the line between the lobsters' eyes and antennae and cut through. Working over a bowl so you catch the juices, twist and break off the claws of the lobsters, then cut off their tails. Cut the bodies in half, following the line down the middle of the back of each lobster. Discard the stomach sac, which is between the eyes and next to the antennae, then remove the tomalley (liver) and roe, if any, and add to the juices in the bowl.

Remove the top shells from the bodies and discard; then remove and discard the lungs (the small saclike appendages on either side of the bodies). Cut each of the bodies, still with small legs attached, in half crosswise, and cut each tail crosswise into 4 medallions. Crack the claws and separate into 2 pieces, breaking them at the joints. (You should have about 1 cup lobster juices, tomalley, and roe.) Add the wine to this mixture and set it aside.

About 15 minutes before serving time, heat the oven to 180 degrees. Heat the oil over high heat in a skillet large enough to hold all the lobster pieces in one layer. Sprinkle the lobster tail and body pieces with the salt and pepper, then dredge in the flour and arrange flat in the hot oil. Cook for about 2 minutes. Turn the pieces over, reduce the heat to low, cover, and continue cooking for about 3 minutes on the other sides, or until the lobster is cooked through. Lift the pieces out of the skillet and place in a serving dish. Keep warm in the oven.

Add the onion, scallions, and garlic to the skillet and cook over high heat, stirring, for about 1 minute. Add the tomato and the reserved lobster juices and bring to a boil. Reduce the heat, cover, and boil gently for 2 minutes, then pour over the lobster, sprinkle with parsley, and serve.

About lobsters

Lobsters are now available year-round in many super-markets and fish stores, so don't consider this a summer dish. In fact, winter lobsters tend to be heavier, with more juicy meat than summer ones. Try to buy female lobsters with roe, since they are usually more tender.

The fastest and most humane way of killing a lobster is to insert the point of a knife at the line between the eyes and antennae. Cutting through the lobster here severs the spinal cord and kills it instantly.

Little shrimp casseroles

This couldn't be simpler. Toss shrimp with garlic, scallions, and mushrooms, top with crumbs, and bake. It's a perfect party dish: you can do the advance preparation hours ahead, and the individual gratins mean no serving up at the last minute. (Of course, you can make this in one large dish.)

I use large shrimp here, but smaller shrimp can be substituted and the cooking time reduced by a few minutes.

4 servings

Mix the butter in a large bowl with the garlic, scallions, mushrooms, salt, pepper, and 1 tablespoon of the oil. Add the shrimp and toss to mix well. Divide the mixture among four individual gratin dishes with about a 1-cup capacity, or spoon into one large gratin dish or a shallow baking dish.

In another bowl, toss the bread crumbs with the remaining 1 tablespoon oil, so that they are lightly coated but still fluffy. Sprinkle the crumbs over the shrimp mixture and pour the wine on top.

About 30 minutes before serving time, heat the oven to 425 degrees. When the oven is ready, place the gratin dishes or dish on a cookie sheet and bake for 10 minutes, or until the topping is nicely browned and the shrimp are just cooked through. Serve immediately.

4 tablespoons (½ stick) unsalted butter, melted

2 teaspoons chopped garlic

¼ cup minced scallions

½ cup coarsely chopped white button mushrooms (about 2 mushrooms)

½ teaspoon salt

½ teaspoon freshly ground black pepper

2 tablespoons canola oil

1 pound large shrimp (about 24), shelled

1 cup fresh bread crumbs (from about ¾ slice white bread processed in a food processor)

¼ cup dry white wine

◄┼ MAKE AHEAD

The shrimp can be tossed with a mixture of garlic, scallions, mushrooms, salt, pepper, and oil a few hours ahead, and the gratins cooked at the last moment in a hot oven.

Stuffed scallops on mushroom rice

You can also make this dish with most butterflied fish steaks, from salmon to halibut. The mushroom rice goes well with poultry or meat. ❧ *4 servings*

Bring about 2 cups water to a boil in a small saucepan. Add the garlic, pine nuts, and basil and boil for 20 to 30 seconds. Drain in a sieve and cool under cold running water.

Chop the garlic, nuts, and basil to make a fine puree and add ⅛ teaspoon of the salt.

Remove and discard the sinew, if any, from the side of each scallop. Split the scallops almost in half horizontally, keeping them hinged together on one side, and open them like a book. Place about 1 teaspoon of the basil puree in the center of each opened scallop and squeeze the scallop halves around the filling.

Spread the oil on a plate. Arrange the scallops on the plate so that they are lightly oiled on one side, then turn to oil lightly on the other sides.

Meanwhile, for the rice: Heat 1 tablespoon of the oil in a medium saucepan over low heat. Add the onion, thyme, and mushrooms and cook for 2 minutes. Add the rice, mix well, then add the stock, salt, and pepper.

Bring to a boil over high heat, then reduce the heat to low, cover, and cook for 20 minutes.

A few minutes before serving time, sprinkle the scallops with the remaining ⅛ teaspoon salt. Heat a stainless steel or aluminum skillet (not nonstick) over high heat until it is very hot. Add the scallops in one layer and cook them for 1 minute on each side,

1 small garlic clove, cut into 4 pieces

1 tablespoon pine nuts

1 cup (loosely packed) fresh basil leaves, with 5 or 6 leaves reserved for garnish

¼ teaspoon salt

8 very large sea scallops (diver scallops; about 12 ounces total)

½ tablespoon good olive oil

Mushroom rice

2 tablespoons good olive oil

¾ cup finely chopped onion

1 teaspoon fresh thyme leaves

½ cup diced (½-inch) wild or white button mushrooms

¾ cup Arborio rice

1 cup chicken stock, homemade (see page 55), or low-salt canned chicken broth

About ½ teaspoon salt (less if using canned chicken broth)

¼ teaspoon freshly ground black pepper

1 tablespoon unsalted butter

2 tablespoons freshly grated Parmesan cheese

or until they are nicely browned. Remove from the heat. Let them rest, covered, in the hot pan while you finish the rice.

Add the remaining 1 tablespoon olive oil to the rice along with the butter and Parmesan cheese. Mix gently. Shred the reserved basil leaves coarsely.

To serve, divide the rice among four plates. Arrange 2 scallops on top of the rice on each plate, sprinkle with the basil, and serve immediately.

◄← MAKE AHEAD
    The rice can sit, covered, in a
    warm place for 15 to 20 minutes before
    you add the butter and cheese.

Rigatoni and mussels with saffron

Saffron lends a depth of mysterious flavor to this pasta and shellfish dish that belies the speed of its preparation. Mussels are great to cook because they don't toughen like cooked clams do, and they also render a lot of juice. For richer flavor, I like to finish the pasta in the mussel juices just before serving.

Although purists object to serving cheese with pasta and shellfish, at my house we sprinkle grated Parmesan or pecorino cheese on top. ❧ *4 servings*

Bring the mussels and wine to a boil in a nonreactive (stainless steel) saucepan over high heat. Boil, covered, for 5 to 6 minutes, until the mussels have opened, tossing them gently after 2 to 3 minutes to move them around in the pan. Drain in a colander set over a bowl. Allow the liquid to sit for a few minutes, then carefully pour it into another bowl, taking care to leave the sediment behind. (You should have about 2 cups mussel liquid; add water if necessary.) Remove the mussels from the shells (reserving a few shells for decoration, if you like), and put them in a bowl.

Heat the olive oil in a large stainless steel skillet or saucepan over high heat, add the onion, garlic, scallions, and celery, and sauté for about 1 minute. Stir in the mussel liquid and cook gently for about 5 minutes. (You should have about 2 cups.) Crumble in the saffron, stir in the mussels, add the salt and pepper, and set aside.

When ready to cook the pasta, bring about 3 quarts salted water to a boil in a large saucepan or pot. Add the pasta and cook until just tender, 12 to 14 minutes. Drain in a colander, then add to the mussel mixture. Bring to a boil and boil for 1 minute.

Serve in soup plates or bowls, sprinkled with cheese and chives, if desired.

4 pounds mussels, well scrubbed
½ cup dry white wine
⅓ cup good olive oil
1 cup chopped onion
2 teaspoons chopped garlic
½ cup minced scallions
½ cup diced (½-inch) celery
1 teaspoon saffron threads (or more, if desired)
½ teaspoon salt
½ teaspoon freshly ground black pepper
12 ounces rigatoni

Garnish

⅓ cup freshly grated Parmesan cheese (optional)
2 tablespoons minced fresh chives (optional)

◄─ **MAKE AHEAD**
The mussels can be prepared a couple of hours ahead, refrigerated, and combined at the last minute with the freshly cooked pasta.

Poultry

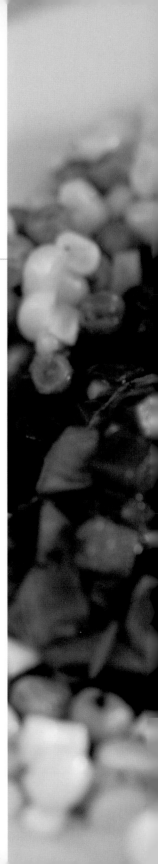

Chicken breasts with garlic and parsley

In France, the classic way of cooking frog's legs is to dredge them in flour, sauté them over high heat in oil and butter and finish them with garlic and parsley and some fresh lemon juice. I've replaced the frog's legs with cubes of chicken breast. Make sure that you dry the cubes well with paper towels before you season them, and don't dredge them in the flour until just before sautéing. Finely milled Wondra flour will give you the crispest coating on the chicken; substitute all-purpose if you must. If possible, prepare this dish in a 12-inch skillet (preferably nonstick), which is large enough to accommodate the chicken in one layer.

4 servings

- 3 boneless, skinless chicken breast halves (each about 7 ounces), cut into 1- to 1½-inch cubes
- 2 tablespoons Wondra flour
- ½ teaspoon salt
- ½ teaspoon freshly ground black pepper
- 2 tablespoons good olive oil
- 1 tablespoon chopped garlic
- 3 tablespoons chopped fresh parsley
- 2 tablespoons unsalted butter
- 1 lemon, quartered

Dry the chicken cubes with paper towels and toss them with the flour, salt, and pepper in a bowl. Heat the oil in a 12-inch skillet over high heat until very hot but not smoking, add the chicken cubes, and cook in one layer, turning occasionally, for about 3½ minutes. Meanwhile, combine the garlic and parsley in a small bowl. Add the butter and the parsley mixture to the skillet and sauté for 1 minute longer, shaking the skillet occasionally to coat the chicken.

To serve, divide among four plates, add a wedge of lemon to each plate, and serve within 15 minutes.

About chicken breasts

Organic chickens are now available in many markets. They are superior in taste and texture.

Chicken on mashed cauliflower with red hot salsa

I particularly like the texture of cauliflower when it is coarsely chopped, as it is here. Cooked and seasoned with butter, it pairs nicely with moist chicken breasts. The salsa–olive oil sauce, spooned over the chicken just before serving, adds color and zest to the dish.　　　 *4 servings*

Bring about 1½ cups water to a boil in a nonreactive (stainless steel) saucepan. Add the cauliflower florets, cover, and cook over high heat for 10 to 12 minutes, until very tender. Drain off the water and add 2 tablespoons of the butter and ¼ teaspoon each of the salt and pepper. Using a knife, cut through the cauliflower in the pan to coarsely chop it. Set aside until serving time.

About 10 minutes before serving time, sprinkle the chicken breasts with the remaining ½ teaspoon each salt and pepper. Arrange the breasts in a single layer in a skillet and add the remaining 1 tablespoon butter and the water. Bring to a boil, cover tightly, and cook over medium to low heat for 3 to 4 minutes. Remove from the heat, and set aside, covered, for 3 to 4 minutes longer to finish cooking while you make the sauce.

For the sauce: Mix the salsa with the olive oil and salt in a bowl. Pour whatever juices have collected around the chicken into the bowl and stir into the sauce.

Reheat the cauliflower in a microwave oven or on the stove, then divide it among four plates. Cut the chicken breast pieces in half and arrange 2 halves on top of the cauliflower on each plate. Coat with the sauce. Sprinkle with the chives and serve.

1 small cauliflower head, white and with tight stalks (about 1 pound), green leaves removed and head separated into florets

3 tablespoons unsalted butter

¾ teaspoon salt

¾ teaspoon freshly ground black pepper

4 boneless, skinless chicken breast halves (each about 6 ounces)

3 tablespoons water

Red salsa sauce

½ cup Red Hot Salsa (page 41) or fresh store-bought salsa

1 tablespoon good olive oil

⅛ teaspoon salt

2 tablespoons chopped fresh chives

Suprême of chicken with balsamic vinegar and shallot sauce

Here I cook chicken breasts fast so they remain moist. A balsamic vinegar sauce lifts their flavor.

In place of the colorful side dish of corn and peas, you could serve a starch, such as potatoes or pasta, or other vegetables, such as string beans or spinach. *4 servings*

Heat the oven to 180 degrees. Heat 1 tablespoon of the butter and the oil over high heat in a heavy saucepan or skillet large enough to hold the chicken breasts in one layer. When hot, add the chicken breasts, and sprinkle them with the salt and pepper. Sauté, uncovered, for about 3 minutes on each side. Transfer the breasts to an ovenproof plate, reserving the drippings in the pan, and place them in the oven and continue cooking for at least 10 minutes but no more than 30 minutes.

Add the shallots and mushrooms to the drippings in the pan, and cook for about 1 minute over high heat. Add the vinegar and ketchup and continue cooking for another minute. Add the water, and cook until the liquid is reduced by half. Add the remaining 1 tablespoon butter, and stir until it is incorporated.

Meanwhile, for the corn and peas: Heat the butter and olive oil in a large skillet over high heat. Add the corn, peas, salt, and pepper. Sauté for 3 to 4 minutes, until the vegetables are cooked through.

To serve, arrange a ring of vegetables on each of four plates. Cut each breast in half crosswise on a slant and place the breast pieces in the center of the vegetables. Coat the chicken with the sauce, sprinkle with the chives, and serve.

2 tablespoons unsalted butter
1 tablespoon good olive oil
4 boneless, skinless chicken breast halves (each about 6 ounces)
¼ teaspoon salt
¼ teaspoon freshly ground black pepper
⅓ cup chopped shallots
1 cup diced (½-inch) white button mushrooms
¼ cup balsamic vinegar
1 tablespoon ketchup
½ cup water

Corn and peas

2 tablespoons unsalted butter
1 tablespoon good olive oil
About 2 cups corn kernels (from 3–4 ears corn)
1½ cups fresh or frozen peas (choose baby peas if using frozen)
¼ teaspoon salt
¼ teaspoon freshly ground pepper
1 tablespoon chopped fresh chives

Chicken tonnato

Inspired by the famous Italian dish *vitello tonnato* (veal in tuna sauce), my chicken tonnato is made with skinless, boneless breasts poached in a vegetable broth and served on a bed of arugula. The sauce is made in seconds in a food processor. Canned tuna (preferably in oil) is the main ingredient in the sauce, which also includes anchovies, mustard, and lemon juice. The delicious poaching broth is served as a soup accompaniment. Any leftover chicken tonnato makes a great sandwich (the recipe follows).

4 servings

For the chicken: Combine the onion, leek, mushrooms, carrot, celery, salt, pepper, and water in a large saucepan (preferably stainless steel). Bring to a boil, reduce the heat to medium-low, and boil gently for 5 minutes. Add the chicken breasts and cook them just until the broth returns to a boil, about 4 minutes. Boil for about 15 seconds, then remove the pan from the heat, cover, and let the breasts stand in the broth for 12 to 15 minutes.

Meanwhile, for the tuna sauce: Set aside 4 of the anchovies for the garnish. Put the tuna and the remaining anchovies in a food processor, along with the oil from both of the cans. Add the egg yolk, mustard, lemon juice, water, salt, and Tabasco and process for a few seconds. With the processor running, add the olive oil in a slow stream and process for a few seconds, or until it is well incorporated and the sauce is smooth.

At serving time, divide the arugula among four plates. Remove the chicken breasts from the broth with a slotted spoon. Cut each breast into 4 crosswise slices, and arrange the slices on top

Chicken

- ½ cup sliced onion
- ½ cup sliced leek, washed well
- 1 cup sliced white button mushrooms
- ½ cup diced carrot
- ½ cup diced celery
- 1 teaspoon salt
- ¼ teaspoon freshly ground black pepper
- 5 cups water
- 4 boneless, skinless chicken breast halves (each about 6 ounces)

Tuna sauce

- 1 (2-ounce) can anchovy fillets in oil
- 1 (3-ounce) can tuna (preferably in oil)
- 1 large egg yolk
- 1 tablespoon Dijon-style mustard
- 1 tablespoon fresh lemon juice
- 1 tablespoon water
- ¼ teaspoon salt
- ¼ teaspoon Tabasco sauce
- ½ cup extra-virgin olive oil

- 4 cups (loosely packed) arugula leaves, washed and dried
- 1 tablespoon drained capers
- 1 tablespoon minced fresh chives

of the arugula. Generously coat the chicken with the tuna sauce and top each serving with 1 of the reserved anchovy fillets. Sprinkle on some capers and chives and serve at room temperature. Reheat the broth, divide among four bowls, and serve with the chicken.

Chicken tonnato sandwich

≈ 1 sandwich

Toast the bread, then spread about 1½ tablespoons of the tuna sauce on each slice. Arrange the chicken on 1 of the slices, top with the arugula, and finish with the tomato slices. Top with the other slice of bread, sauce side down. Trim off the crusts, if you like, cut the sandwich in half, and serve.

2 slices bread (about 2½ ounces total)

3 tablespoons leftover tuna sauce

4 thin slices chicken

½ cup (loosely packed) arugula

4 thin slices tomato

Chicken bouillabaisse

This dish, made with chicken, kielbasa, and potatoes, takes its inspiration from the famous fish stew of the South of France and contains all the classic seasonings, including saffron. An expensive spice, saffron is essential to this dish. The best comes from Spain. I've also added a little tarragon at the end. Although not absolutely necessary, tarragon has a slight anise taste that complements the other seasonings. To reinforce its flavor, I add a splash of Pernod or Ricard at the last minute, although this ingredient is optional. I serve my chicken bouillabaisse with a traditional rouille, a garlicky mayonnaise seasoned with cayenne and paprika.

Yes, there are lots of ingredients in this recipe, but it's quick to assemble and cooks in about 30 minutes. It makes a meal in itself when followed by a salad and some cheeses.

⤙ 4 servings

For the bouillabaisse: Mix the olive oil, garlic, saffron, lemon zest, salt, pepper, fennel seeds, herbes de Provence, onion, celery, and carrot in a large bowl. Add the chicken and turn to coat. Cover and refrigerate until you are ready to cook.

Transfer the contents of the bowl to a stainless steel pot and add the tomatoes, wine, water, and potatoes. Cover, bring to a boil over high heat, then reduce the heat to low and boil gently for 25 minutes. Add the sausage and cook for 5 minutes longer. If adding Pernod, stir it in now with the tarragon.

For the rouille: Remove half a cooked potato and ¼ cup liquid from the pot and place in a food processor with the garlic, cayenne, and paprika. Process for 10 seconds. Add the egg yolk.

Bouillabaisse

- 1 tablespoon good olive oil
- 1 tablespoon coarsely chopped garlic
- ½ teaspoon saffron threads
- 1 teaspoon grated lemon zest
- ¾ teaspoon salt
- ½ teaspoon freshly ground black pepper
- ¼ teaspoon fennel seeds
- ¼ teaspoon herbes de Provence
- ½ cup coarsely chopped onion
- ¼ cup coarsely chopped celery
- ¼ cup coarsely chopped carrot
- 4 chicken thighs (about 1¾ pounds total), skin and fat removed
- ½ (14½-ounce) can diced tomatoes (about 1 cup)
- ½ cup dry white wine
- ¾ cup water
- 5 red or Yukon Gold potatoes (about ¾ pound total), peeled and halved
- 1 piece (about 10 ounces) kielbasa sausage, cut into 4 pieces
- 2 teaspoons Pernod or Ricard (optional)
- 1 tablespoon chopped fresh tarragon, chives, or parsley

Then, with the processor running, slowly pour in the oil and process for a few seconds, or until incorporated. Taste for salt and add, if needed.

Serve the bouillabaisse in warmed soup plates with a spoonful of the rouille drizzled on top.

Rouille

- 2 large garlic cloves
- ⅛ teaspoon cayenne pepper
- ¼ teaspoon paprika
- 1 large egg yolk
- ½ cup extra-virgin olive oil
  Dash of salt, if needed

◄◄ **MAKE AHEAD**
The chicken can be combined with the herbs and vegetables up to 8 hours in advance.

Sautéed quail with raita

With their slightly gamy flavor, quail is the ideal choice for the cook looking to move beyond chicken. These tiny birds, which cook very quickly, are served here with a cooling and refreshingly spicy raita. It sets them off perfectly.

The raita can also be served with broiled, roasted, or grilled chicken or other poultry, on its own as a salad, or as a first course on lettuce. You can have the quail as a first course, allotting one per person.

4 servings

Mix the olive oil, cumin, and cayenne in a large shallow dish. Add the quail and turn to coat well with the mixture. Cover and refrigerate.

For the raita: Combine all the ingredients in a small bowl and set aside until serving time. (You will have about 1½ cups.)

At serving time, heat the oven to 180 degrees. Heat a nonstick skillet over high heat until very hot. Sprinkle the quail with the salt and sauté over high heat for about 2 minutes on each side, or 3 minutes if you are planning to serve it immediately. Transfer to an ovenproof dish and place in the oven to rest for 10 to 20 minutes before serving. Serve with the raita.

About quail

Quail are available in some supermarkets, but if yours doesn't have them, purchase them at gourmet stores, Asian markets, or online. Sometimes you can buy them fresh, but often they are frozen; either will work for this recipe. Most of the time quail come boned—at least the central carcass is removed—and these are what I use here, although you can use unboned quail. The birds can marinate in the oil and seasonings for up to a day before cooking, or they can be rubbed with these ingredients at the last minute.

◄+ MAKE AHEAD

The quail can be cooked and placed in a 180-degree oven for up to 30 minutes before serving.

The raita can be made a day ahead and refrigerated.

2 tablespoons good olive oil
1 teaspoon ground cumin
½ teaspoon cayenne pepper
8 quail (4–5 ounces with bones, 3–4 ounces boned)
¾ teaspoon salt

Raita

1 cup peeled, seeded, and diced (¼-inch) cucumber
1 cup good whole-milk yogurt (preferably Greek)
2 tablespoons finely chopped fresh spearmint or peppermint
½ teaspoon salt
1 teaspoon Asian-style hot chili oil (more or less, depending on taste) or wasabi powder
½ teaspoon chopped garlic

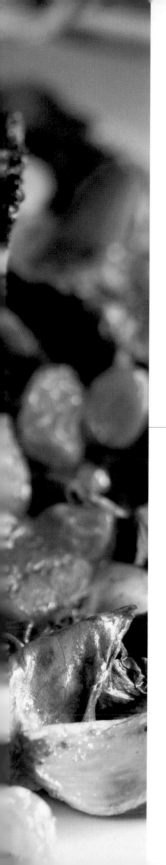

Meat

Instant beef tenderloin stew

This stew consists of pieces of tender steak that are sautéed for a few minutes—just until rare—and then added to an array of vegetables. The stew is best done with beef tenderloin, although New York strip steak, sirloin tips, and skirt steak are also tender enough to use. This recipe can also be made with lamb: trim any fat and cut the meat into 1½-inch pieces. The meat is prepared in one skillet and the vegetables in another; they are combined at the last moment.

4 servings

2 tablespoons unsalted butter

1 tablespoon good olive oil

1½ cups diced (½-inch) potato, rinsed under cold running water

1 cup baby carrots (about 4 ounces)

1 cup small white button mushrooms (about 2 ounces)

⅓ cup chopped onion

1 tablespoon chopped garlic

½ cup baby peas, fresh or frozen

½ teaspoon salt

¼ teaspoon freshly ground black pepper

1 pound beef tenderloin, trimmed of all fat and cut into 1½-inch pieces

2 tablespoons dry white wine

2 tablespoons chicken stock, homemade (see page 55), or low-salt canned chicken broth

Heat 1 tablespoon of the butter and the olive oil in a large skillet over medium-high heat. Add the potatoes, carrots, and mushrooms. Cook, partially covered, stirring occasionally, for about 8 minutes, or until the vegetables are cooked through and lightly browned. Add the onion and cook for 1 to 2 minutes longer. Add the garlic, peas, and ¼ teaspoon of the salt and cook for 1 minute. Set aside, covered, while you cook the steak.

Heat the remaining 1 tablespoon butter in another skillet over medium-high heat until it is very hot but not smoking. Sprinkle the remaining ¼ teaspoon of salt and the pepper on the fillet pieces and add the meat to the skillet in one layer. Sauté, turning, for 2 to 3 minutes, until the meat is browned on all sides. Transfer to a platter. Add the wine and stock to the skillet and boil for about 10 seconds. Arrange the meat, vegetables, and juices on four warmed plates and serve immediately.

Beef short rib, mushroom, and potato stew

Meat stews can be prepared very quickly in a pressure cooker; the meat becomes tender in about 30 minutes, compared to the nearly 2 hours required by conventional cooking. Dried shiitake mushrooms, broken into pieces and added to the stew without soaking, become chewy and full flavored as they cook, almost like meat. ❧ *4 servings*

Remove any surface fat and sinews from the short ribs. Place them in a pressure cooker with the oil and brown over high heat for about 8 minutes, turning occasionally, until well browned on all sides. Remove from the heat and pour off any fat.

Add the mushrooms, then the remaining ingredients, except the parsley, and cover tightly with the pressure-cooker lid. Cook over high heat until the gauge indicates that the stew is cooking on high pressure. Reduce the heat to maintain the pressure and cook for 30 minutes.

Decompress the pressure cooker according to the manufacturer's instructions (I do mine in the sink so that the steam is contained somewhat as it is emitted). Open the pressure cooker and taste the stew for seasonings, adding additional salt and pepper if needed. Divide the stew among four warmed soup plates, sprinkle with the parsley, and serve immediately.

2 pounds beef short ribs (4 ribs), as lean and meaty as possible

1 tablespoon canola oil

8 dried shiitake mushrooms, stems removed and caps broken in half

12 small Yukon Gold potatoes (about 1 pound total), peeled or unpeeled

1½ cups chopped (1-inch) onions

3 garlic cloves, peeled

2 bay leaves

2 sprigs fresh thyme or ½ teaspoon dried thyme

1½ teaspoons salt

½ teaspoon freshly ground black pepper

1 cup dry white wine

½ cup water

1 tablespoon chopped fresh parsley

◄┼ **MAKE AHEAD**
The stew can be made a day ahead and reheated for an even more flavorful result.

About pressure cookers

The pressure cooker is an essential piece of equipment at my house. My wife, Gloria, often cooks dried beans and makes stews in it. There are several makes and models on the market, all with slight differences, so follow the manufacturers' instructions when using them.

A pressure cooker is especially helpful at high elevations, where water boils at lower temperatures. A couple of degrees are lost per 1,000 feet of elevation. In Aspen, for example, water boils at around 196 degrees, a temperature that is often not high enough to break down the cellulose in beans and meat. A pressure cooker raises the boiling temperature to 250 degrees, rather than 212 degrees, the temperature at which water boils at sea level. This softens the fibers of meat, beans, and other foods, cooking and tenderizing the food much faster than conventional cooking methods.

Veal roast

Yes, a roast of veal can be fast. Prepared in a pressure cooker (see page 159) and flavored with only salt and pepper, thyme, and an onion, this one takes only about 40 minutes.

A shoulder roast of veal is best for this recipe; unfortunately, there are as many names for this cut as there are butchers. It may be called a veal clod, a flatiron, or a top blade-under-blade roast. Whatever its name, it makes a moist, tender, and flavorful roast. When you get it from the butcher, remove any thick layers of fat from the top.   ⋟ *6 servings*

Heat the butter in a pressure cooker. Meanwhile, salt and pepper the roast and place it in the hot butter with the quartered onion. Brown over medium to high heat for about 10 minutes, turning occasionally, until browned on all sides. Add the herb sprig and cover tightly with the pressure-cooker lid. Cook over high heat until the gauge indicates that the roast is cooking on high pressure. Reduce the heat to low, and cook for 30 minutes.

Decompress the pressure cooker according to the manufacturer's instructions (I do mine in the sink so that the steam is contained somewhat as it is emitted). Open the pressure cooker and let the roast rest for a few minutes before carving it. Serve with the juices and onion quarters.

1 tablespoon unsalted butter

½ teaspoon salt

1 teaspoon freshly ground black pepper

1 3-pound shoulder veal roast

1 large onion (about 8 ounces), peeled and quartered

1 large sprig fresh thyme, oregano, or rosemary

Ham steaks with apricot-mustard glaze

Ready to eat in 30 minutes, this main dish is good company fare. I use a fair amount of Tabasco sauce in my cooking, but the quantity can be reduced to suit your taste.

4 servings

Line a cookie sheet with a double layer of aluminum foil. Mix the apricot jam, sugar, mustard, and Tabasco in a small bowl. Heat the broiler.

Trim off and discard the outer edges of the ham steaks if they are tough. Place the steaks on the cookie sheet, divide the glaze between or among them, and spread it evenly over the top of each. Broil about 6 inches from the heat source for 10 to 12 minutes, until the tops of the steaks are brown and bubbly. Let rest for 5 to 10 minutes, then cut each steak into 2 pieces if necessary and serve.

2 tablespoons good apricot jam

1½ tablespoons brown sugar

2 tablespoons Dijon-style mustard

1 teaspoon Tabasco sauce

2 ham steaks (each 7 by 5 inches and about ½ inch thick; about 1½ pounds total) or 4 individual ham steaks (each about ½ inch thick; about 1½ pounds total)

Breaded pork scaloppine with mushroom sauce

Pork tenderloins are lean, tender, moist, and low in calories. In this recipe, I slice the tenderloin, pound the slices into scaloppine (which could not be easier), bread them, and serve with a mushroom pan sauce. You can do this with chicken breast or veal too.   *4 servings*

Heat the oven to 180 degrees. Cut the tenderloin crosswise into 8 slices, each about 1½ ounces. Pound the slices until they are about ¼ inch thick, then sprinkle them with ¾ teaspoon of the salt and the pepper.

Beat the egg thoroughly with a fork in a shallow bowl. Combine the bread crumbs and the cheese in another shallow bowl. Dip the slices of meat into the egg to lightly coat each side, let the excess drip off, and dip the meat into the mixture until well coated on each side. Arrange the breaded meat on a platter.

At cooking time, divide the olive oil between two nonstick skillets and heat until hot but not smoking. Arrange 4 scaloppine in each skillet so that they don't overlap and sauté over high heat for about 1½ minutes on each side, or until nicely browned. Arrange on a clean platter, and keep warm in the oven.

Add the butter and onion to one of the skillets and sauté over high heat for 1 minute, or until slightly softened. Add the mushrooms and the remaining ½ teaspoon salt and sauté for 2 to 3 minutes, until the mushrooms are lightly browned and most of their liquid has evaporated.

Spoon the mushrooms over the scaloppine, sprinkle with the chives and lemon juice, and serve.

¾ pound pork tenderloin, trimmed of fat
1¼ teaspoons salt
½ teaspoon freshly ground black pepper
1 large egg
3 slices white bread, processed into crumbs (about 2 cups)
2 tablespoons freshly grated Parmesan cheese
3 tablespoons good olive oil
2 tablespoons unsalted butter
¼ cup chopped onion
2½ cups sliced white button mushrooms
1 tablespoon minced fresh chives
Juice of ½ lemon

◄ MAKE AHEAD
The meat can be pounded and breaded 5 to 6 hours ahead, covered, and refrigerated until cooking time.

Pork chops with zesty sauce

Since the flavor of lean pork chops is a bit bland, I like to pair them with something spicy and juicy. ❧ *4 servings*

For the sauce: Mix the ingredients in a small bowl.

For the pork chops: Trim the pork chops of any fat. Heat the oven to 180 degrees.

Heat the butter with the olive oil in a heavy skillet over high heat until hot. Sprinkle the meat with the salt and pepper and add to the skillet. Cook for about 4 minutes on each side, or until nicely browned. Arrange the meat on an ovenproof platter and keep it warm in the oven.

Add the vinegar to the drippings in the skillet and cook over high heat for about 1 minute to reduce and mellow the vinegar. Add the onion, scallions, garlic, and tomato and cook for about 2 minutes over high heat. Add the sauce and boil for 1½ to 2 minutes over high heat. Stir in the olives and any juices the meat has rendered and bring back to a boil. Coat the chops with the sauce and serve immediately.

Zesty sauce

- ¼ cup water
- 3 tablespoons chili sauce
- 1 teaspoon Tabasco sauce
- 2 teaspoons soy sauce
- 1 teaspoon A1 steak sauce

Pork chops

- 4 lean boneless pork loin chops (each about 8 ounces and about 1 inch thick)
- 1 tablespoon unsalted butter
- 1 tablespoon good olive oil
- ¾ teaspoon salt
- ¾ teaspoon freshly ground black pepper
- ¼ cup red wine vinegar
- ½ cup chopped onion
- ⅓ cup minced scallions
- 2 teaspoons chopped garlic
- 1 cup diced (1-inch) tomato
- ¼ cup pitted Kalamata olives

About pork

For braising or stewing, I always use shoulder chops with a fair amount of fat. For quick cooking, however, I like to use loin chops. Choose the leanest chops you can find, and trim off whatever fat is left before cooking. Without the fat, the meat should cook rapidly to a very slightly pink center. The meat is done when the internal temperature is between 155 and 160 degrees. If overcooked, lean meat gets tough and chewy.

Thirty-minute cassoulet

The famous cassoulet of southwest France features white beans, roast pork, sausage, and duck or goose. Assembled in a cast-iron or earthenware casserole, it is usually covered with bread crumbs and takes hours—sometimes days—to prepare.

In my version, I use ham, canned cannellini beans, and Italian and bratwurst sausages and serve the stew on a large platter, home style. Even considering the time required to remove the plastic covering and the tough outside skin from the ham, it doesn't take more than 30 minutes to prepare from start to finish. *4 to 6 servings*

Heat the olive oil in a large skillet and add the ham and Italian sausage.

Cover and cook over high heat for 7 to 8 minutes, turning occasionally. Add the bratwurst, mushrooms, onion, garlic, thyme, and bay leaf. Mix well and cook for 5 to 6 minutes. Add the beans, tomato, water, and pepper, bring back to a boil, reduce the heat to low, cover, and boil gently for 5 minutes.

At serving time, discard the bay leaf, cut the ham into slices and the sausage pieces in half, and arrange the meat on a platter with the beans. Sprinkle the parsley on top. Serve with the Tabasco and mustard.

1 tablespoon good olive oil

About 1 pound rolled shoulder ham (also called daisy ham or Boston butt), tough outer skin removed

About ¾ pound hot Italian sausages, cut into 3-inch pieces (about 6 pieces)

4 bratwurst sausages (about 1 pound)

1 cup diced (½-inch) whole button mushrooms (about 3 ounces)

¾ cup diced (½-inch) onion

2 tablespoons crushed garlic (about 4 large cloves)

½ teaspoon dried thyme leaves

1 bay leaf

2 (15½-ounce) cans cannellini beans, drained and rinsed under warm running water

¾ cup diced (1-inch) tomato (1 large plump tomato)

½ cup water

¼ teaspoon freshly ground black pepper

3 tablespoons coarsely chopped fresh parsley

For serving

Tabasco sauce

Dijon-style mustard

Sausage and potato packet

Baking the stew in an aluminum foil packet makes it especially easy and eliminates the cleanup. This is a great winter "picnic" dish. *4 servings*

Heat the oven to 425 degrees. Arrange a piece of heavy-duty aluminum foil about 18 inches wide by 36 inches long on a cookie sheet so that half of the foil covers the pan and the remainder extends beyond it at either end. Pour the olive oil over the foil covering the pan, then rub the onion halves in the oil to coat them. Distribute the potatoes and garlic around the onions and sprinkle with the salt. Finally, scatter the sausages throughout the vegetables and place the rosemary on top. After making certain that the ingredients are in one layer in the foil on the pan, fold the foil overhang over the mixture and fold in the sides to secure the stew in a tight casing.

Bake the foil package for 1 hour. Using potholders, transfer the package from the pan to a platter. Open the foil carefully, sprinkle the stew with the parsley, and serve directly from the package.

1 tablespoon good olive oil

4 medium onions (about 1 pound total), cut crosswise into halves

12 small Yukon Gold potatoes (about 1 pound total), peeled or unpeeled

About 16 garlic cloves, unpeeled

½ teaspoon salt

6 Italian sausages (about 1 pound total), 3 hot and 3 sweet

1 pound kielbasa sausage, cut into 4 pieces

2 sprigs fresh rosemary

1 tablespoon chopped fresh parsley

Broiled lamb chops with spinach

Thick double lamb chops are good grilled, sautéed, or broiled, as here. Raisins, pimientos, garlic, and olive oil are staples of Spanish cuisine, and my sautéed spinach brings these tastes together. If double lamb chops are not available, serve two 1-inch-thick chops per person; broil them for about 2½ minutes per side for medium-rare.

4 servings

For the lamb chops: Line a cookie sheet with a double layer of aluminum foil. Pour the oil onto the foil and spread it evenly over the surface. Heat the broiler.

Mix together the paprika, cumin, salt, and pepper in a small bowl and rub the mixture onto both sides of the lamb chops. Press the chops onto the oiled sheet, and then turn them over, so they are oiled on both sides.

Broil about 6 inches from the heat source for about 5 minutes on one side. Turn the chops over and cook for about 3 minutes on the other side for medium-rare. Let rest for 4 to 5 minutes while you prepare the spinach.

For the spinach: Heat the olive oil in a large skillet over high heat, then add the garlic and sauté for about 15 seconds. Add the spinach and press it down into the hot skillet. Using tongs, stir the spinach so that the slices of garlic are mixed with the spinach and don't burn underneath it. After about 1 minute, the spinach will be wilted.

Add the raisins, pimientos, salt, and pepper and sauté the spinach, turning occasionally, for 2 minutes longer, or until completely soft. Serve with the lamb chops.

Lamb chops

- 2 teaspoons good olive oil
- ½ teaspoon paprika
- ½ teaspoon ground cumin
- ½ teaspoon salt
- ½ teaspoon freshly ground black pepper
- 4 thick (each about 2 inches) lamb loin chops, trimmed of any surrounding fat (about 1½ pounds total)

Spinach

- 3 tablespoons good olive oil
- 2 tablespoons sliced garlic
- 1 pound spinach, large stems removed, washed and dried
- ⅓ cup golden raisins
- ⅓ cup diced (½-inch) pimientos
- ½ teaspoon salt
- ¼ teaspoon freshly ground black pepper

◂◂ MAKE AHEAD
The spinach can be prepared 1 to 2 hours ahead and reheated in the microwave.

Pressure-cooker lamb and white bean stew

This stew has a lot of liquid, which makes it an ideal vehicle for dunking bread or serving with boiled rice or Couscous (page 107). Don't reduce the amount of water in the recipe; the beans will not cook properly if there is too little water. ✎ *6 servings*

Put all the ingredients in a pressure cooker, cover tightly with the pressure-cooker lid, and cook over high heat until the gauge indicates that the stew is cooking on high pressure. Reduce the heat to low and cook the stew for 40 minutes.

Decompress the pressure cooker according to the manufacturer's instructions (I do mine in the sink so that the steam is contained somewhat as it is emitted). Open the pressure cooker and let the stew rest for a few minutes until the fat rises to the surface. Spoon off and discard as much fat as possible and taste the stew for seasonings, adding more salt and pepper as needed. Serve hot.

4 shoulder lamb chops (about 2 pounds total), trimmed of fat

1½ cups (about ½ pound) dried white beans, such as navy or great northern, picked over and washed under cold running water

2 cups canned diced tomatoes

1 cup diced (1-inch) onion

1 cup diced (1-inch) trimmed and washed leek

2 tablespoons coarsely chopped garlic

1 sprig fresh thyme and 1 sprig fresh sage, or 1 teaspoon herbes de Provence

1½ teaspoons salt

1 teaspoon freshly ground black pepper

2 teaspoons Worcestershire sauce

3 cups cold water

Desserts

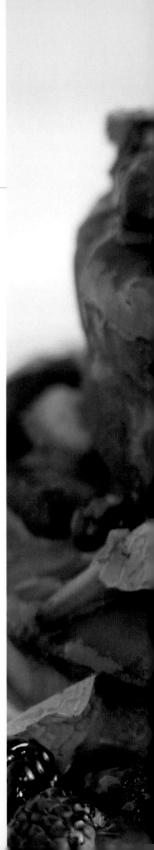

Almond cake with berries

This food processor cake is moist and tender. Before serving, the cake is brushed with whiskey-laced syrup, then covered with jam-flavored fruit, and served with sour cream or crème fraîche. To make a three-layer cake like the one in the photograph, see the variation that follows.

Almond paste is available in most supermarkets in 8-ounce cans or tubes. ✌ *6 to 8 servings*

Heat the oven to 350 degrees. Put the almond paste, sugar, butter, and vanilla in a food processor and process for about 10 seconds. Add the eggs, milk, and salt and process for 5 seconds. Add the flour and baking powder and process for 5 to 10 seconds, or until smooth.

Butter an 8-inch round cake pan (2 inches deep) with the reserved ½ teaspoon butter. Pour the cake batter into the pan and bake for 45 minutes. Cool on a rack.

At serving time, place the cake on a serving platter.

For the syrup: Combine the ingredients in a small bowl. Using a spoon or pastry brush, moisten the cake with the syrup. Scatter the berries on top of and around the cake. Spoon on the diluted apricot jam and garnish with the mint leaves. Serve with the crème fraîche or sour cream.

4 ounces almond paste (⅓ cup tightly packed)

¾ cup sugar

8 tablespoons (1 stick) unsalted butter, ½ teaspoon reserved to butter the cake pan

1 teaspoon pure vanilla extract

3 large eggs

¼ cup milk

Dash of salt

1 cup cake flour (5–6 ounces)

½ teaspoon baking powder

Syrup

3 tablespoons water

3 tablespoons whiskey, rum, or cognac

¼ cup sugar

Garnish

1½ pounds berries (raspberries, blueberries, strawberries, blackberries) or other available fruits (currants, diced dried peaches, or diced dried apricots)

½ cup good apricot jam, diluted with ⅔ cup water

8–10 fresh mint leaves

1 cup sour cream or Crème Fraîche (page 200), for serving

Variation

To make a large cake for a special occasion—birthday, wedding, or the like—triple the recipe and bake in different-size cake pans, perhaps 12 inch, 8 inch, and 5 inch. Brush the largest layer with one third of the syrup, center the second largest layer on top and brush with one third of the syrup, and top with the smallest cake layer. Brush with the remaining syrup and scatter the berries over the layers. Spoon the diluted apricot jam over the berries and cake and garnish with the mint leaves and/or edible flowers. Serve with the crème fraîche or sour cream.

◅← **MAKE AHEAD**

You can make the cake early in the day. Or make several cakes and wrap them well for the freezer. Defrost, still in their wrappings, in the refrigerator.

Big almond macaroons with apricot filling

The small cans or tubes of almond paste found in the baking section of most supermarkets make this a cinch. These macaroons are larger than conventional ones, and one "sandwich" per person is a good dessert. You can vary the filling with other jams. ⬱ *6 servings*

1 (8-ounce) can or tube almond paste

¾ cup sugar

1 extra-large or jumbo egg white

2 tablespoons good apricot or peach preserves

2 tablespoons unsweetened cocoa powder

Heat the oven to 375 degrees. Line a large cookie sheet with a reusable nonstick cooking mat or parchment paper.

Put the almond paste and sugar in a food processor and process for 10 to 12 seconds. Add the egg white and process for 6 to 8 seconds, until the mixture becomes smooth and creamy.

For each cookie, spoon about 1½ tablespoons of the macaroon mixture onto the cookie sheet. Make 12 cookies in all and space the mounds evenly. With a moistened finger, press lightly on each mound to smooth the top.

Bake the macaroons for 20 minutes, or until they are nicely browned and have a cracked surface. Remove the cookie sheet from the oven and place on a rack. Let cool, undisturbed, for about 15 minutes, then remove the cookies with a spatula.

Spread 1 teaspoon of the preserves on the flat side of one of the macaroons, and press another macaroon on top, flat side down. Repeat with the remaining macaroons, spreading half of them with the preserves and pressing a plain macaroon on top of each to create 6 sandwiches. Sprinkle some of the cocoa on the top surface of each macaroon sandwich, coating it well.

Put the macaroons in a container with a tight-fitting lid, and, for best results, refrigerate until serving time. Serve 1 macaroon sandwich per person.

Apple skillet cake

Gloria makes a great pancake that she serves with honey. I used a variation on her recipe for this cake batter and added sautéed apples. Some of the cooking is done on the stovetop, and the dessert is finished under the broiler and dusted with confectioners' sugar. Although I make the cake in a skillet, it can also be prepared in a decorative pie plate and served directly from the plate.

↝ *4 servings*

Melt the butter in a 10- to 12-inch ovenproof nonstick skillet. Arrange the apple wedges in one layer in the skillet and sprinkle them with the granulated sugar. Cook over medium to low heat for about 5 minutes, then turn the wedges over and cook them on the other side for 5 minutes longer. Set the apples aside in the skillet until ready to finish the dessert.

Meanwhile, for the batter: Place all the ingredients in a food processor and process for a few seconds to combine.

When ready to cook, heat the broiler. Pour the batter over the apples in the skillet. Cover and cook over low heat on top of the stove for 6 to 8 minutes. Uncover the skillet and broil about 6 inches from the heat source for 6 to 8 minutes, until nicely browned on top. Invert onto a serving plate. Sprinkle with the confectioners' sugar, cut into wedges, and serve. If you like, pass a pitcher of maple syrup at the table.

◄+ MAKE AHEAD

The apples can be cooked ahead, and the batter can be made 30 minutes ahead and refrigerated. It is best to cook the pancake just before serving.

- 3 tablespoons unsalted butter
- 2 medium soft-fleshed apples (preferably Empire or McIntosh), peeled, cored, and cut into 8 wedges each
- 1 tablespoon granulated sugar

Batter

- 1 cup cottage cheese
- ¾ cup sour cream
- 1 teaspoon pure vanilla extract
- 2 tablespoons granulated sugar
- ¾ cup all-purpose flour
- 3 large eggs
- 1 tablespoon confectioners' sugar, for dusting

- 1 cup pure maple syrup (optional), for serving

Caramelized apple–granola timbales

Think of these as individual bread puddings. I combine apples with caramel and fold in pecan granola for crunch and body. These are also ideal for weekend breakfast or brunch.

They are best served lukewarm with a dab of sour cream.

4 servings

⅓ cup plus 1 teaspoon sugar

2 tablespoons water

3 tablespoons unsalted butter

3 apples (preferably Granny Smith or Golden Delicious; about 1½ pounds total), peeled, cored, and cut into 1-inch dice (about 4½ cups)

⅓ cup granola (I use pecan granola)

4 slices firm white sandwich bread

½ cup sour cream, for serving

Put the ⅓ cup sugar and water in a skillet and bring to a boil over high heat, stirring just until the sugar is moistened. Continue boiling without stirring, until the mixture turns into caramel, which will take about 5 minutes, shaking the pan near the end so that the sugar caramelizes without burning around the edges. Add 2½ tablespoons of the butter, and when it has melted, add the apples. Stir well, cover, and cook over medium heat for about 5 minutes, or just until the apples are tender. Add the granola and cook, uncovered, until all the moisture evaporates and the apple mixture sizzles and begins to brown again.

Using a knife or a round cutter, trim the bread slices so that they will fit the tops of four small ovenproof bowls or custard cups with a ¾-cup capacity.

Divide the apple mixture among the ovenproof bowls. Press on the apples to make them fit tightly in the bowls and smooth the tops. Fit one of the bread rounds on top of each bowl, then butter the top surfaces of the bread rounds with the remaining ½ tablespoon butter. Sprinkle with the remaining 1 teaspoon sugar.

When ready to finish the desserts, heat the oven to 400 degrees. Place the timbales on a cookie sheet and bake for about 8 minutes, or until the bread is nicely browned and the apple mixture is warmed through. Unmold while still warm onto dessert plates. Serve with a little sour cream.

⤙ MAKE AHEAD

This dessert can be prepared up to a day ahead and baked in the oven to brown the bread rounds just before serving. Bring to room temperature before cooking.

Apple, pecan, and apricot crumble

For this recipe I cube McIntosh, Rome Beauty, or Macoun apples, so that they cook quickly, and mix them with orange juice to prevent discoloration. This dessert is best served lukewarm with a bit of crème fraîche or sour cream, or even ice cream, if you want to splurge.

4 servings

Mix the apples, apricots, pecans, cinnamon, orange juice, and sugar in a large bowl.

For the topping: Combine the ingredients in a small bowl, working them with your fingers until crumbly and well mixed.

Heat the oven to 400 degrees. Spoon the apple mixture into a 6-cup glass baking dish or gratin dish and sprinkle the crumble mixture on top. Place the dish on a cookie sheet and bake for about 30 minutes, or until the apples are tender when pierced with the point of a knife and the topping is brown and crusty. Serve lukewarm with crème fraîche or sour cream.

2 pounds Rome Beauty, Macoun, and/or McIntosh apples, peeled, cored, and cut into 1-inch pieces (about 5 cups)

¾ cup diced (¾-inch) dried apricots

½ cup broken pecan pieces

½ teaspoon ground cinnamon

½ cup orange juice

⅓ cup sugar

Crumble topping

¾ cup all-purpose flour

1 teaspoon baking powder

⅓ cup sugar

8 tablespoons (1 stick) unsalted butter, at room temperature

½ cup Crème Fraîche (page 220) or sour cream, for serving

Rhubarb and berry crumble

Crumbles, brown betties, crisps, and cobblers are among my favorite American desserts. Rhubarb flourishes in my garden, and in late spring I often combine it with strawberries and sprinkle a crumble crust on top. The addition of spearmint or peppermint leaves, plentiful near my pond, is also a seasonal touch. ✌ *4 to 6 servings*

Heat the oven to 400 degrees. Put the rhubarb and berries in a bowl with ¼ cup of the sugar, 2 tablespoons of the flour, and the mint leaves. Mix well and transfer to a 6-cup-capacity gratin dish or glass baking dish.

Put the remaining ¼ cup sugar and 2 tablespoons flour, the granola, and the butter in a small bowl and combine with your fingers until crumbly and well mixed. Sprinkle over the fruit.

Bake for about 35 minutes, or until the fruit is bubbling and the topping is browned. Serve with the sour cream or crème fraîche.

¾ pound rhubarb, cut into 2-inch pieces (about 3 cups)

¾ pound strawberries, hulled and halved or quartered, depending on size (about 2½ cups)

½ cup sugar

4 tablespoons all-purpose flour

About 24 fresh peppermint or spearmint leaves

1 cup granola (I use pecan granola)

About 5 tablespoons unsalted butter, at room temperature

1 cup sour cream or Crème Fraîche (page 220), for serving

Apple peel granité with apple puree

This refreshing combination of apple puree and granité is a natural pairing, and it's a great way of using the apple skins, which are high in pectin. The puree is good on its own or with a cookie. ❧ *4 to 6 servings*

For the granité: Peel the apples. Set aside the peel from 2 of them for the granité and reserve the peeled apples for the puree. Chop the reserved apple peel in a food processor and put it in a saucepan with the cider and water. Bring to a boil, cover loosely, and boil gently for 25 minutes. (You should have about 2 cups; adjust with water, if necessary.) Add the sugar and mix well to dissolve it. Pour the mixture into a bowl and place in the freezer for a few hours, stirring the mixture occasionally, if you like. When it turns into slush or frozen crystals, it is ready to be served.

For the apple puree: Halve and core the peeled apples and cut the flesh into 2-inch chunks. Put them in a saucepan with the maple syrup, vanilla, and water. Bring to a boil, partially cover, and boil very gently for 10 to 12 minutes, until soft and mushy. Let cool to lukewarm. Add the sour cream and blend with an immersion blender or in a food processor until very creamy. Refrigerate until cool.

At serving time, spoon the apple puree into a glass serving bowl, or divide it among four to six individual glass dessert dishes. Top with the granité and sprinkle on a little Calvados, if you like.

Granité

2 pounds Granny Smith apples (about 4)

2 cups apple cider

2 cups water

2 tablespoons sugar

Apple puree

½ cup maple syrup

1 teaspoon pure vanilla extract

¼ cup water

¼ cup sour cream

About 2 tablespoons Calvados (apple brandy; optional)

↤ MAKE AHEAD

If the granité is solidly frozen, transfer it to the refrigerator about 30 minutes before serving to soften slightly and make it easier to scoop out. The puree will keep in the refrigerator, covered, for a few days.

Crepes with banana-rum filling

There are few desserts that are easier or faster to make than crepes. Four of them cook quickly in a nonstick skillet. Here, I fill them with caramelized bananas.

4 servings

For the crepes: Mix the flour and egg with about ¼ cup of the milk, stirring with a whisk until the batter is smooth. Mix in the remaining ½ cup milk, add the rum, sugar, and salt, and stir until well combined. (You will have about 1⅓ cups.)

Divide the butter into 4 equal pieces. Melt 1 piece of butter in a large (10- or 12-inch) nonstick skillet. When the butter is hot, add about ⅓ cup of the batter, and swirl the pan to coat the bottom. Cook over medium to high heat for about 2 minutes on the first side, or until nicely browned, then turn and cook for 1 minute, or until the second side is well cooked. Repeat with the remaining butter and batter to make 3 additional crepes. Stack the crepes on a plate, cover with plastic wrap, and set aside.

For the caramelized bananas: Put the sugar and 1 tablespoon of the water in a large skillet. Bring to a boil over high heat, stirring just until the sugar is moistened. Continue to cook, without stirring, for about 3 minutes, or until the mixture turns into a caramel, shaking the pan near the end of the cooking period so that the caramel doesn't burn around the edges.

Add the bananas, lemon juice, butter, and the remaining 2 tablespoons water. Cover and cook over medium-low heat for 3 to 4 minutes. Stir to ensure that there are no lumps in the caramel. Let the mixture come to room temperature, then stir in the rum.

Divide the banana mixture among the four crepes, and then fold in the sides to enclose the filling and make 4 compact pack-

Crepes

½ cup all-purpose flour
1 large egg
¾ cup milk
1 tablespoon dark rum
½ teaspoon granulated sugar
  Dash of salt
2 tablespoons unsalted butter

Caramelized bananas

½ cup granulated sugar
3 tablespoons water
3 large bananas (about 1½ pounds total), cut into ½-inch slices (about 3 cups)
3 tablespoons fresh lemon juice
2 tablespoons unsalted butter
1 tablespoon dark rum
1 tablespoon confectioners' sugar
½ cup Crème Fraîche (page 220) or sour cream

ages. Place a package on each of four dessert plates. Alternatively, line each of four dessert plates with a crepe, folding up the edges of each crepe as necessary to make a cup on each plate. Divide the banana filling among the cups. Cover with plastic wrap if not serving immediately.

At serving time, reheat each dessert in a microwave oven for about 1 minute, or until it is lukewarm. Sprinkle with the confectioners' sugar and serve each crepe with 2 tablespoons crème fraîche or sour cream.

◄◄ MAKE AHEAD
The filled crepes can be made a few hours ahead and covered with plastic wrap. The crepes without the filling can be made a day ahead, stacked, covered with plastic, and refrigerated.

Banana bourbon coupe

This is one of those recipes that you prepare on the spur of the moment with whatever is available. I went skiing in Vermont with my good friend Jean-Claude, and we invited some guests for dessert. All we had were a few bananas and some cookies. We mixed some bourbon (of course we had lots of wine and liquor!) with honey and lime juice, tossed in the bananas, and served them over crushed cookies in wide shallow glasses for Champagne (called coupes). The toasted almonds add crunch.   ⌇ *4 servings*

3 tablespoons honey

3 tablespoons bourbon

1 tablespoon fresh lime juice

4 bananas (about 1¼ pounds total)

3 tablespoons sliced almonds

4–6 plain cookies, depending on size, such as store-bought sugar cookies

1 teaspoon lime zest strips or grated lime zest

Combine the honey, bourbon, and lime juice in a bowl. Peel and slice the bananas crosswise into ½-inch-thick slices and toss them in the honey mixture.

Toast the sliced almonds, either by heating them in a skillet set over high heat for a few minutes or by scattering them on a cookie sheet and toasting them in a 400-degree oven for about 6 minutes, or until they are lightly browned and fragrant. Set aside.

At serving time, crush the cookies coarsely and divide the crumbs among four glasses. Spoon the banana mixture on top of the cookies and garnish the desserts with the toasted almonds and lime zest.

Pink grapefruit terrine

The sweet-tart taste of citrus is refreshing at the end of a meal. I use unflavored gelatin to thicken the grapefruit juice, flavor it with honey and mint, and combine it with grapefruit sections in custard cups. The quick sauce is made of orange marmalade thinned with orange juice and Grand Marnier.

🌱 *4 servings*

Peel the grapefruits with a sharp paring knife, cutting closely all around the flesh, removing the skin and white pith. Then cut on either side of each grapefruit segment, remove the segments from the membranes, and put the segments in a bowl. Hold the membranes over a small saucepan and squeeze them to extract the juice. (You should have about 24 grapefruit segments and ¾ cup juice.)

Alternatively, peel off the outer skin and pith and separate the fruit into ordinary segments. Place the store-bought juice in a small saucepan.

Divide the segments among 4 custard cups with a ¾-cup capacity, arranging about 6 in each.

Sprinkle the gelatin over the juice in the pan. Heat over low heat, stirring occasionally, until the gelatin has melted. Add the honey and grenadine and stir well. Mix in the shredded mint leaves and pour the mixture over the grapefruit segments, dividing it evenly. Cover, and refrigerate for at least 3 to 4 hours, or overnight.

Meanwhile, for the orange sauce: Stir the marmalade, Grand Marnier, and orange juice together in a small bowl.

At serving time, dip the bottom of the cups briefly into hot water, then invert them and unmold the desserts onto individual plates. Coat each dessert with a few spoonfuls of the sauce and serve.

2 pink grapefruits (1–1¼ pounds each)

¾ cup store-bought grapefruit juice (if you choose the alternative method and don't remove the grapefruit segments from their membranes)

2 teaspoons unflavored gelatin (about 1 envelope)

2 tablespoons honey

1 tablespoon grenadine syrup

1 tablespoon shredded peppermint or spearmint leaves

Orange sauce

½ cup orange marmalade

2 tablespoons Grand Marnier

2 tablespoons orange juice

↤ MAKE AHEAD

You do need to plan ahead for this dessert. Make it in the morning or the day before.

Grapefruit gratinée

Baking gives the brown sugar–graham cracker crust a warm crunch, which contrasts pleasantly with tart fruit. This is an especially appropriate dessert in winter. ✺ *4 serving*

2 pink grapefruits (about 1 pound each)

4 graham crackers (about 2½ ounces)

¼ teaspoon ground cinnamon

3 tablespoons light brown sugar

1½ tablespoons unsalted butter

Cut a small slice from both ends of each grapefruit so that it will sit upright without tipping over, and cut the grapefruits in half. Using a paring knife, release the grapefruit segments from their membranes by cutting around the fruit.

Heat the oven to 425 degrees. Put the graham crackers, cinnamon, sugar, and butter in a food processor and process for 10 to 15 seconds to make coarse crumbs.

Arrange the cut grapefruit halves in a gratin dish or glass baking dish set on a cookie sheet. Divide the crumb topping among the grapefruit halves and spread it over the surface of each. Bake for about 12 minutes, or until the tops are nicely browned. Serve lukewarm or at room temperature.

◄─ **MAKE AHEAD**

The topping can be made ahead and the grapefruits cooked up to 1 hour before serving.

Chestnut and chocolate cake

This classic, unbaked "cake" is for people who like dense, assertive chocolate desserts. It's super-easy—requiring only moments to combine the chestnut, melted chocolate, and rum—and extremely rich. ≈ *6 to 8 servings*

Oil a rectangular loaf pan with a capacity of 3 to 4 cups. Cut a thin strip of parchment paper (about 12 inches long and 1½ inches wide) and position it in the bottom of the pan so that the ends of the strip run up two opposite ends of the pan and extend a little beyond the edges; this will make the dessert easier to un-mold at serving time. Alternatively, if you don't want to un-mold the dessert, you can use a serving bowl or terrine.

Put the chestnut puree in a large bowl and add the rum, butter, and melted chocolate. Mix thoroughly to combine, then pour into the pan or bowl. Cover with plastic wrap and refrigerate for at least 4 hours (or up to a couple of days).

At serving time, unmold the cake onto a serving platter and cut it into 6 to 8 slices or spoon it out of the bowl. Spoon some crème fraîche or sour cream over each slice and serve.

About chestnut puree

Cans of pureed chestnuts flavored with vanilla and sugar come from the South of France and are available in specialty and gourmet markets. This puree is also wonderful served on its own or over ice cream.

¼ teaspoon vegetable oil, for oiling the pan

1 (1-pound) can chestnut spread or puree flavored with sugar and vanilla

2 tablespoons dark rum

4 tablespoons (½ stick) unsalted butter, at room temperature

8 ounces bittersweet chocolate, melted

1 cup Crème Fraîche (page 220) or sour cream

≈← **MAKE AHEAD**

You do need to plan for this dessert: it needs to chill for at least 4 hours. It can be made a day ahead.

Chocolate hazelnut brownie cake

One of my favorite—if not my absolute favorite—American dessert is brownies. In this sinfully luscious version, the brownie is transformed into a thin round cake with an intense chocolate flavor. At serving time, I pile on whipped cream flavored with orange zest and Grand Marnier.

8 servings

Heat the oven to 350 degrees. Line an 8- or 9-inch tart or round cake pan with aluminum foil and butter the foil with ½ teaspoon of the butter.

Break the chocolate into small pieces and put it into a microwavable glass bowl with the remaining butter. Microwave for about 1 minute on high, then leave undisturbed in the microwave oven for about 5 minutes. Reheat again on high for 1 minute. (If the chocolate is heated for 2 or 3 consecutive minutes in the microwave, it tends to scorch.) Remove from the microwave and stir until smooth.

Scatter the hazelnuts on a cookie sheet and toast for 5 to 6 minutes, or until they are lightly browned (there's no need to remove the skins). Cool for a few minutes, then transfer to a plastic bag and crush into very small pieces with a rolling pin or a small pan.

Put the sugars, eggs, and vanilla into a large bowl and beat with a whisk until smooth. Add the nuts and melted chocolate and fold in gently with a rubber spatula until well incorporated. Pour into the tart pan and bake for about 20 minutes, or until the cake is just set but still wet in the center. (A toothpick inserted in the center will come out with wet crumbs.) Cool to room temperature on a rack. (The cake will set as it cools.)

For the garnish: Put all the ingredients except the mint in a mixing bowl and whip gently with a whisk or electric mixer until the cream holds firm peaks.

Pile the cream on top of the cake, garnish with the mint, and cut into wedges to serve.

Variation

For more conventional brownies, bake the batter in an 8-inch square pan and cut into squares for serving.

Cake

- 5 tablespoons unsalted butter
- 6 ounces bittersweet or semisweet chocolate
- ½ cup shelled hazelnuts
- ½ cup light brown sugar
- ½ cup granulated sugar
- 2 large eggs
- 1 teaspoon pure vanilla extract

Garnish

- 1 cup heavy cream
- 1½ tablespoons granulated sugar
- 1 tablespoon Grand Marnier
- 1 teaspoon grated orange zest
- 5 or 6 fresh mint leaves

◂◂ MAKE AHEAD

The cake can be made up to 24 hours ahead and refrigerated. Set it out at least 1 hour before serving to achieve the proper soft texture, or reheat it for a few minutes in a low oven.

Hasty pudding with apricot sauce

Here is my tribute to an old-fashioned American dessert. This pudding is sweetened with sugar and scented with lemon and vanilla. Unlike the traditional American version, it takes only minutes to prepare. These puddings are a common dessert in French households, and I made them often for my daughter when she was small. Serve it with cookies, if you like.   *4 servings*

2 cups half-and-half
⅓ cup semolina
½ cup sugar
2 teaspoons grated lemon zest
2 teaspoons pure vanilla extract
¼ cup sour cream

Apricot sauce

2 tablespoons sliced almonds
⅓ cup good apricot jam
3 tablespoons Armagnac, cognac, or brandy
1 tablespoon fresh lemon juice

Bring the half-and-half to a boil in a medium saucepan. Add the semolina, mix well with a whisk, and bring back to a boil. Reduce the heat to very low and boil very gently, stirring often with the whisk, for 2 to 3 minutes, until creamy and thick but still pourable. Remove from the heat, add the sugar, lemon zest, and vanilla, and mix well. Stir in the sour cream. Transfer the pudding to a serving bowl, cool to room temperature, and cover.

For the sauce: Heat the oven to 400 degrees. Toast the almonds on a cookie sheet for 4 minutes, or until light brown and fragrant. Combine the remaining ingredients and the almonds in a bowl.

At serving time, spread the sauce on top of the pudding and serve.

Variations

For a leaner pudding, use milk instead of half-and-half, and for the richest possible pudding, cook the semolina in cream.

You can substitute cinnamon for the lemon zest.

For accompaniments, you can substitute another fruit sauce, such as the Orange Sauce on page 190. Or serve with Crème Fraîche (page 220) or sour cream.

◄← MAKE AHEAD
This pudding is best served cool or cold, so plan accordingly. It can be made a day ahead.

Warm chocolate cakes with apricot-cognac sauce

There are many recipes for flourless warm chocolate cakes, some simple to make, some complicated. In this simplest possible version, the cakes are cooked in the muffin-size aluminum foil cups with paper liners available at any supermarket, making them easy to unmold and eliminating messy cleanup chores. ❧ *4 servings*

For the chocolate cakes: Heat the oven to 350 degrees. Put the chocolate, butter, sugar, cornstarch, and vanilla in a microwavable glass bowl. Microwave for 1 minute, then let rest for 2 to 3 minutes. If the mixture is not melted, microwave again for 30 seconds to 1 minute, just until melted. Mix with a whisk until smooth, then add the whole eggs and egg yolks and whisk again until smooth.

Place four foil muffin-size cups, each with a paper liner inside, on a cookie sheet. Divide the batter among the cups. Bake for about 8 minutes, then remove from the oven. At this point the desserts will be bubbly and still liquid in the centers. Let cool to lukewarm or room temperature. The desserts will continue cooking, but their centers will remain creamy.

For the sauce (if making): Mix the ingredients in a bowl until smooth.

At serving time, remove the foil from the chocolate cakes and peel off the paper liners. Turn the desserts so that they are right side up and serve 1 per person on a dessert plate with a spoonful of the apricot-cognac sauce or a dollop of sour cream in the center.

Chocolate cakes

- 4 ounces bittersweet or semisweet chocolate (chocolate chips or morsels, or larger pieces of chocolate broken into ½-inch pieces)
- 4 tablespoons (½ stick) unsalted butter
- 1 tablespoon sugar
- 1 teaspoon cornstarch
- 1 teaspoon pure vanilla extract
- 2 large eggs
- 2 large egg yolks

Apricot-cognac sauce (optional)

- ¼ cup good apricot jam
- 1 tablespoon water, if the jam is very thick
- 1 tablespoon cognac
- ½ cup sour cream, if not using sauce

⤙ **MAKE AHEAD**

The desserts should be cooked about 45 minutes ahead so that they are lukewarm when served. If cooked further ahead, reheat them for a few minutes in a conventional oven or for a few seconds in a microwave oven.

Pinot noir granité

The clean taste of this bracing concoction is perfect after a heavy meal. Make it with the wine you like best and, for a variation, serve it with fresh berries or cherries.

✺ 4 servings

Combine the water with the sugar and honey in a medium bowl and mix well to dissolve the sugar. Add the lime juice, grenadine, and wine and pour into a gratin dish or glass baking dish. Freeze for 2½ to 3 hours, stirring occasionally, if you like. When it turns to slush or frozen crystals, it is ready to be served. Serve in chilled glasses with an edible flower or a strip of lime zest on top of each dessert, and a cookie, if you like.

½ cup hot water
⅓ cup sugar
1 tablespoon honey
¼ cup fresh lime juice
2 tablespoons grenadine syrup
2 cups good Pinot Noir
A few edible flowers or strips of lime zest, for garnish (optional)
Plain cookies, for serving (optional)

◄◄ **MAKE AHEAD**

The granité can be tightly covered and solidly frozen. Transfer it to the refrigerator about 30 minutes before serving to soften slightly and make it easier to scoop out.

Raspberries with balsamic vinegar

Balsamic vinegar gives wonderful complexity to berries, especially if you use a good aged one. This recipe can also be prepared with an equal amount of lime or lemon juice instead of the vinegar. Serve with Sugar Cookie Bread (opposite page) if you like. ❧ *4 servings*

1½ tablespoons good balsamic vinegar (preferably aged)

2 tablespoons sugar

2 (12-ounce) containers fresh raspberries (about 2½ cups total)

About 8 strips lemon zest, for garnish (optional)

In a medium bowl, thoroughly mix the vinegar and sugar. Add the berries and toss gently, so as not to damage them.

Spoon into glasses or small, deep dishes for serving and garnish each serving with a few strips of lemon zest, if desired.

◄+ MAKE AHEAD

Do not combine these ingredients more than a few hours ahead or the raspberries will become mushy.

Sugar cookie bread

This is a great way to use leftover bread, either regular white slices or country-style. Wonderfully crisp, these "cookies" can be served in place of biscotti with fruit desserts. You can vary them by adding cinnamon or by substituting brown sugar for the granulated sugar. They are excellent with fruit desserts, especially Raspberries with Balsamic Vinegar (opposite page). ❧ *4 servings*

4 slices white bread, crusts removed

2 tablespoons unsalted butter, at room temperature

2½ tablespoons sugar

Heat the oven to 300 degrees. Spread both sides of the bread with the butter. Sprinkle the sugar on a nonstick cookie sheet, and press the buttered bread slices in the sugar, turning them so that they are coated on both sides with the sugar. Cut each bread slice into 3 strips on a cutting board, then return the strips to the cookie sheet and bake for 10 minutes. Turn the strips over and bake for 10 minutes longer. The bread should be very crusty and nicely browned.

Store the cookie bread in a plastic container with a tight-fitting lid until ready to serve.

◂+ MAKE AHEAD

The cookies will stay crisp for 2 days in an airtight container.

Two raspberry gratins

One of my all-time favorite desserts, raspberry gratins are a cinch to make if you have frozen, unsweetened raspberries on hand, as I always do, and good store-bought cookies. I give two variations: one is made with packaged chocolate chip cookies—who doesn't love the combination of chocolate and raspberries?—and one with buttery shortbread. (I use Mrs. Fields individually wrapped boxed chocolate chip cookies and Walkers Pure Butter Shortbread from the supermarket, although other brands—or even homemade cookies—can be substituted.)

The chocolate chip cookies are best crumbled by hand rather than in a food processor, which would puree them. The shortbread can be crumbled in the food processor, or you can place in a plastic bag and crush it with the bottom of a small skillet or a rolling pin. Serve the gratins lukewarm or at room temperature, with or without sour cream, as you like.

Chocolate-raspberry gratins

≈ *4 servings*

Heat the oven to 375 degrees. Divide the frozen berries among four small (1-cup) gratin dishes or custard cups.

Toss the crumbled cookies and sugar together in a small bowl. Divide the crumbs among the gratin dishes, sprinkling them evenly over the berries, and dot with the butter. Arrange the dishes on a cookie sheet and bake for 16 to 18 minutes, until nicely browned on top and the berries are bubbling. Let cool to lukewarm or room temperature, and serve with sour cream, if you like.

- 2 cups IQF (Individually Quick Frozen) unsweetened raspberries (about 8 ounces)
- 1½ cups crumbled chocolate chip cookies (4–6 cookies)
- ¼ cup sugar
- 2 tablespoons unsalted butter
- ½ cup sour cream (optional)

Shortbread-raspberry gratins

≈ *4 servings*

Heat the oven to 375 degrees. Divide the frozen berries among four small (1-cup) gratin dishes or custard cups.

Toss the crumbled shortbread and sugar together in a small bowl. Divide the crumbs among the gratin dishes, sprinkling them evenly over the berries, and dot with the butter. Arrange the dishes on a cookie sheet and bake for 16 to 18 minutes, until nicely browned on top and the berries are bubbling. Let cool to lukewarm or room temperature, and serve with sour cream, if you like.

- 2 cups IQF (Individually Quick Frozen) unsweetened raspberries (about 8 ounces)
- 1½ cups crumbled shortbread cookies (8–10 cookies)
- ¼ cup sugar
- 2 tablespoons unsalted butter
- ½ cup sour cream (optional)

Strawberry panachée

A panachée is a mixture of two or more ingredients with different colors, flavors, or shapes. For this one, I mix fruits and fruit puree with cookies and cream. It takes only a few minutes to prepare and almost any berries will work. I like to serve these desserts in shallow glass bowls or goblets. Although any cookies will do, I prefer to use Scottish shortbread cookies in this dessert.

I tend to reserve the centers of the strawberries for slicing. I puree the tops and the bottoms, always a little less ripe, in a food mill. Any berry jam will work fine, and sour cream or crème fraîche makes a good garnish. ⫰ *4 servings*

Cut off the bottom and top of each berry. (You should have about 1¼ cups of tops and bottoms.) Slice the centers of the berries and set aside. Push the berry tops and bottoms and the jam through a food mill or process in a mini food processor until pureed. Mix the sliced berries into the puree. Cover with plastic wrap, and refrigerate until ready to serve.

At serving time, put the cookies in a plastic bag and crush them coarsely with a rolling pin. Divide the crumbs among four glass bowls or goblets. Spoon about half of the berry mixture on top of the cookies. Stir the crème fraîche or sour cream to loosen it and spoon on top of the berries. Top with the remaining berry mixture. Garnish each dessert with a mint sprig, and, if you like, pass some crème fraîche or sour cream.

2½ cups ripe strawberries
¼ cup jam (raspberry, currant, or strawberry are good)
4 shortbread cookies
⅓ cup Crème Fraîche (page 220) or sour cream, plus additional for serving
4 sprigs fresh mint or basil

⫰ **MAKE AHEAD**
The sliced berries and puree can be made a few hours ahead and kept covered in the refrigerator.

Oranges and cream cheese

When Gloria tasted this orange and cream cheese combination, she was immediately reminded of the desserts her Puerto Rican mother made when she was a child.

4 servings

Mix the cream cheese and sugar in a bowl until thoroughly blended and set aside. Using a zester, remove about 2 teaspoons zest from one of the oranges and set aside. Or, if you don't have a zester, grate an equivalent amount of zest from the orange.

Peel all the oranges with a sharp paring knife, cutting closely all around the flesh, removing the skin and white pith. Remove each segment from its membrane by cutting as close to one membrane as you can with your knife, then twisting the knife upward at the core and cutting up alongside the next membrane. Continue until all the segments have been removed. Squeeze the membranes from each orange over a bowl and reserve the juice. (You will have about ½ cup.)

Alternatively, peel off the skin and pith and separate the fruit into ordinary segments. Pour the store-bought juice into a small bowl.

Add the marmalade to the juice and mix well.

Break the pomegranate, if using, into chunks and, using a spoon, tap on the skin sides of the chunks over a bowl of cool water to make the seeds fall out. Reserve the seeds and discard the pulpy flesh. (You should have about ¼ cup seeds.)

At serving time, divide the cream cheese mixture among four soup plates and arrange the orange segments on top. Pour the juice and marmalade sauce over and around the oranges. Sprinkle with the pomegranate seeds, if using, and the orange zest, and serve.

1 cup whipped cream cheese

¼ cup sugar

4 seedless oranges (8–10 ounces each)

½ cup store-bought orange juice (if you choose the alternative method and don't remove the oranges from their membranes)

½ cup orange marmalade

1 medium pomegranate (optional)

Pears in honeyed wine

Poached fruits are always welcome for dessert, especially after a heavy meal. I particularly like to poach pears because they hold their shape well and are always available at the supermarket. Anjou, Bartlett, and Comice pears usually cook faster than Bosc or Seckel pears. Be sure to select pears that are at the same stage of ripeness so that they cook in the same amount of time.

A little ice cream is a bonus that enriches this dessert, which can be served with cookies, if you like. *4 servings*

- 2 very large Bosc pears (about 1½ pounds total)
- 1 cup sturdy, fruity red wine (Rhône Valley is a good choice)
- ¼ cup grenadine syrup
- ⅓ cup honey
- 1 pint vanilla ice cream

Peel the pears, cut them into quarters, and core. Put the pear pieces in a saucepan, add the wine, grenadine, and honey, and bring to a boil. Cover, reduce the heat to low, and boil gently until the pears are tender when pierced with the point of a knife, about 15 minutes. (Riper pears will cook faster, and harder, less ripe pears may take up to 30 minutes to become tender.)

Remove the pears from the cooking liquid with a slotted spoon or skimmer and put them in a bowl. Boil the liquid over high heat until it is reduced to about ¾ cup. (This will take about 10 minutes.) Pour the syrup over the pears in the bowl and cool.

Serve 2 wedges of pear per person in a dessert dish with some of the syrup and a small scoop of the ice cream.

Caramelized peaches

I always keep a few cans of peaches in my pantry to use as a last-minute dessert or as a garnish for chicken or duck. The caramel cream sauce—made from the syrup in the can—makes this dessert particularly luscious.

4 servings

Drain the peaches, reserving the syrup, and pour the syrup into a skillet. Cook over high heat until the syrup is reduced and turns into caramel, 9 to 10 minutes, shaking the pan near the end so the caramel doesn't burn around the edges.

Add the peaches to the caramel and stir in the cream. Bring to a boil, stirring occasionally, to melt the caramel and combine it with the cream. Boil for 1 to 2 minutes, then transfer to a bowl and cool. Stir in the cognac and lemon juice and add the water if the sauce is too thick. Cover and refrigerate until serving time.

At serving time, toast the brioche slices and place a slice on each of four dessert plates. Arrange 2 peach halves on top of each slice and coat with the sauce. Sprinkle on the pistachios.

1 (29-ounce) can peach halves in heavy syrup (about 8 peach halves and 1 cup syrup)

½ cup heavy cream

1 tablespoon cognac

1 tablespoon fresh lemon juice

1–2 tablespoons water, if necessary

4 slices (½-inch-thick) brioche or pound cake

2 tablespoons coarsely crushed pistachio nuts

◄← MAKE AHEAD

This dessert is best chilled, so that the caramel sauce has a luxurious texture. Make it early in the day or just before dinner.

Peaches with peach sauce

Save this recipe for full summer, when yellow and white peaches are in season. If the peaches you select are firm, peel them with a good vegetable peeler; if they are soft, use a sharp knife. Cookies or pound cake is a nice accompaniment. *4 servings*

Mix the lemon juice, preserves, and brandy, if using, in a small bowl. Roll the peeled peaches in the sauce and refrigerate if not serving immediately.

To serve, place a peach in each of four dessert bowls and pour the sauce over the peaches. Garnish each serving with a sprig of mint.

2 tablespoons fresh lemon juice

½ cup good peach or apricot preserves

1 tablespoon pear brandy (optional)

4 large ripe but firm peaches, either yellow or white (about 2 pounds total), peeled

4 sprigs fresh mint

MAKE AHEAD

This recipe is best prepared at the last minute to prevent the peaches from discoloring. If you're preparing the dessert ahead, be sure to cover the peaches with the sauce; the lemon juice in it will prevent discoloration.

Pineapple wedges in caramel

You can make this in a skillet on the stovetop in just a few minutes. Dark rum lends a wonderful flavor to the pineapple, but if you prefer not to use alcohol, the recipe is quite good without it.　　　　　*4 servings*

Cut off the green top and base from the pineapple and cut the pineapple lengthwise into 8 wedges. Remove the core and skin from the wedges.

Heat the butter, brown sugar, and orange juice in a large skillet over medium heat, stirring just until the sugar is moistened. Add the pineapple wedges in one layer, bring to a boil, cover, and cook for 6 to 7 minutes without stirring. Uncover, turn the wedges in the pan, and continue to cook, uncovered, for 6 to 8 minutes, shaking the pan near the end, until the syrup in the skillet turns into a thick, dark caramel. Turn the wedges in the caramel, and transfer the contents of the skillet to a gratin dish or serving platter. When lukewarm, sprinkle with the rum and pistachio nuts, if you like, and serve at room temperature with sour cream and cookies, if desired.

1 small pineapple (about 2½ pounds with green top)

3 tablespoons unsalted butter

⅓ cup brown sugar

½ cup orange juice

2 tablespoons dark rum (optional)

Crushed pistachio nuts, for garnish (optional)

Sour cream (optional), for serving

Plain cookies (optional), for serving

◂← MAKE AHEAD
This dessert can be prepared early in the day and refrigerated, although I prefer it at room temperature.

Pear brown betty

Here's a great way to use leftover baked goods, from cakes with cream to cookies. Be sure to adjust the amount of cinnamon and butter you add according to what baked goods you choose; when using rich pastries, I cut back on these ingredients, but when I use crumbled cookies and cubed bread, I increase them to get the proper result. ✀ *4 servings*

Heat the oven to 400 degrees. Drain the pears, reserving 1 cup of the syrup. Cut each pear half into 6 pieces. Put the broken pieces of pastry or bread into a bowl and mix in the pear pieces, reserved syrup, butter, raisins, and cinnamon. Transfer the mixture to a 4- or 5-cup glass baking dish or gratin dish and bake for 40 to 50 minutes, until nicely browned on top. Serve lukewarm with a heaping tablespoon of crème fraîche or sour cream on each serving.

1 (29-ounce) can pear halves in heavy syrup (about 6 pear halves)

4 cups (about 10 ounces) coarsely broken pieces of leftover croissants, muffins, scones, Danish pastries, and/or bread

2 tablespoons unsalted butter, melted

⅓ cup golden raisins

1 teaspoon ground cinnamon
About ½ cup Crème Fraîche (page 220) or sour cream, for serving

Mock tiramisù

Any dessert with cake or cookies soaked in syrup and coated with cream, such as English trifle or Italian tiramisù, has a place on my table. When I was a kid, one of my aunts made a delicious dessert with hard butter cookies that she soaked in coffee and served with crème fraîche and sugar on top.

This simplified version of tiramisù could not be easier to make. Ladyfingers and mascarpone, a creamy cheese, are available in most supermarkets, but if you can't find mascarpone, substitute an equal amount of whipped cream cheese. ❧ *4 servings*

For the filling: Put the mascarpone, sour cream, sugar, and vanilla in a medium bowl and mix gently with a whisk until smooth.

For the syrup: In another bowl, combine the coffee, rum, and sugar.

Arrange the ladyfingers in one layer in a glass baking dish or gratin dish large enough to accommodate them in one layer and pour the syrup evenly over them.

Spoon about one quarter of the cream filling into a 3- to 4-cup glass bowl. Add one third of the ladyfingers, pushing them into the filling. Spoon in another one quarter of the cream and add another layer of ladyfingers. Repeat with another one quarter of the cream and the remaining ladyfingers, then pile the remaining cream filling on top. Smooth the surface and sprinkle with the cocoa powder.

Cover and refrigerate for at least 1 hour. At serving time, plunge a spoon deep into the mixture to get multilayered servings and divide among four dessert plates.

Cream filling

- 1 cup mascarpone cheese (8 ounces)
- 1 cup sour cream (8 ounces)
- ¼ cup sugar
- 1 teaspoon pure vanilla extract

Syrup

- 1 cup strong brewed coffee
- 2 tablespoons dark rum
- 1 tablespoon sugar

- 3 ounces ladyfingers (12 or 24, depending on the brand)
- 1 teaspoon unsweetened cocoa powder

◄← MAKE AHEAD

This is best chilled for at least 1 hour.

Vanilla praline dessert

This delicious dessert is made in moments with ready-made products from the supermarket. Buy good ice cream, and make sure you move it from the freezer to the refrigerator at least one hour before serving.

There are hundreds of cookies available at the market. I selected Pepperidge Farm's Bordeaux butter cookies, but any variety you fancy will work. ✎ *4 servings*

1 pint good vanilla ice cream
About ½ cup Nutella hazelnut spread
8 small cookies (see headnote), broken into pieces
2 tablespoons pistachio nuts

Move the ice cream from the freezer to the refrigerator 1 hour before serving to soften.

At serving time, place the Nutella in a microwave oven and heat for 1 to 1½ minutes, until the spread is soft and pourable.

Spoon about ¼ cup of the softened vanilla ice cream into four dessert bowls. Cover with the broken cookies, dividing the pieces among the servings, then pour about 2 tablespoons of the hazelnut spread on top. Spoon another ¼ cup ice cream over the spread in each dish and sprinkle the pistachio nuts on top. Serve immediately.

About Nutella

Hazelnut spread, which is sold as Nutella, is available in most supermarkets. It is similar to *pralin,* or praline paste, made of roasted hazelnuts and caramel and used in all French pastry shops. Nutella comes plain or flavored with cocoa; I like the plain one best for this recipe, but the cocoa-flavored version can be used. I heat the jar of Nutella directly in a microwave oven until it reaches the proper consistency to pour over the ice cream.

Champagne on fruit "rocks"

The "rocks" here are frozen cubes of pureed berries and fruit juices. Served with Champagne or a sweet dessert wine, such as Sauternes or Beaumes-de-Venise, they make a special cocktail—an elegant ending to any meal. Serve with a slice of pound cake or a few plain cookies.

❧ 4 servings

Defrost the berries overnight in the refrigerator. Push the berries and the jam through a food mill fitted with a fine disk into a bowl. If you want the puree to be seedless, strain again through a strainer. (You will have about 1⅓ cups.)

Pour the berry puree into ice cube trays to make 12 cubes. Pour the fruit juice into another 12-cube tray. Freeze for a few hours, or until frozen.

Pry the cubes out with a small paring knife and return them to the freezer in a plastic bag until ready to use.

About 30 minutes before serving, put 2 or 3 juice and berry cubes in each of four glasses. Place the glasses in the refrigerator for 30 minutes or on the counter for 15 minutes to soften the cubes slightly. Pour the wine over the cubes, and serve with the cake or cookies.

Variation

The berry cubes are delicious, but you can omit them. Use just the fruit juice cubes.

1 (12-ounce) package IQF (Individually Quick Frozen) unsweetened raspberries

⅓ cup blackberry preserves (preferably seedless)

About 1⅓ cups orange juice, cranberry juice, or another juice of your liking

1 bottle Champagne, or ½ bottle dessert wine, such as Sauternes or Beaumes-de-Venise

Pound cake or cookies, for serving

◄◄ **MAKE AHEAD**

You do need to plan, since the berries have to defrost and the "rocks" have to freeze, but this dessert is easy enough to prepare in the morning or the night before.

Remember to put the fruit cubes into their glasses and in the refrigerator about 30 minutes before you pour in the wine, so that the cubes soften slightly.

Crème fraîche

Traditional crème fraîche begins life as cream with a high fat content. Fermentation thickens it and gives it a distinctive tang. It is available in some supermarkets and specialty stores but is sometimes difficult to find. This recipe duplicates the flavor but is much leaner.   ≈ *about 1 cup*

1 cup sour cream
⅓ cup heavy cream, whipped for about 30 seconds with a whisk

Gently stir the sour cream and whipped cream together in a bowl. Cover and refrigerate for up to 1 hour before serving.

Author's Acknowledgments

The production of this cookbook and the PBS series that it accompanies required the concerted effort of many capable people. Although I can't thank everyone involved in these two projects here, I would like to mention the names of a few individuals whose enthusiasm and assistance were especially helpful.

The book would not have been possible without the love and support of my wife, Gloria, who uncomplainingly tastes my food and occasionally suggests a change or addition that makes a dish better. Thanks, too, to Norma Galehouse, my assistant; this is the eighteenth book we've worked on together, and I continue to rely on her ability to transform my handwritten recipes into a manuscript.

I am grateful to Doe Coover, my agent, who always manages to find precisely the right publisher for my books.

I want to thank Roy Finamore and Houghton Mifflin's Rux Martin, both of whom served ably as senior editors on this book; their guidance and sound advice shaped and refined it. I also want to thank the copy editor, Virginia McRae, whose keen attention to detail is an essential part of the publishing process. The attractive jacket is the handiwork of Michaela Sullivan, and Ralph Fowler did a great job with the book's interior design.

I am indebted to Ben Fink for his superlative photography throughout. His sharp, clear pictures of my finished dishes illustrate our shared vision to make the freshly prepared food the focal point of every photo in the book. Thanks also to Shannon O'Hara, Ben's gifted assistant, who was so helpful in smoothing the progress of the photography sessions. Also indispensable at the photo shoots were Maryann Pomeranz and Andrea Albin, both students at the French Culinary Institute in New York City, who graciously helped with the cooking and cheerfully cleaned up the kitchen afterward.

The television series based on the book, filmed at KQED-TV in San Francisco, required the cooperation and help of a multitude of people. I am most grateful to John Boland, KQED's executive vice president, Danny McGuire, the executive producer of the series, and Michael Isip, the executive director of television poduction and programming, for supporting my vision of fast food and seeing the project through from beginning to end.

For her insight, dedication, and hard work, I am indebted to my good friend and producer, Susie Heller. She dealt with all the complexities associated with the filming and resolved any and all problems as they occurred with consummate professionalism and good humor. Thanks, too, to Bruce Franchini, our talented and unflappable director and friend, who got the best possible close-ups of the food we cooked.

Once again I am grateful to Jolee Hoyt, our unit manager on this and earlier series; her financial wizardry kept us all on track. My thanks also to Kris Ravetto, whose makeup artistry enabled me to look my best day after day during the taping.

Without the expertise of our operations/technical crew, the series *Jacques Pépin Fast Food My Way* would never have seen the light of day. My heartfelt thanks go out to Frank Carfi, Ernie Neumann, Kim McCalla, Steve Welch, Lee Young, John Andreini, Randy Brase, Margaret Clarke, Mike Van Dine, Dean Gaskill, Lynton Vandersteen, Helen Silvani, Harry Betancourt, Greg Overton, and Mike Elwell. Their combined efforts helped make this project a success.

The shows require the utmost support and cooperation of my friends in the back kitchen, and I want to thank Laura Pauli, our competent and conscientious chef, for her excellent work. In addition, I am gratified by the great work of five capable volunteers: Jason Mecum, Doug Whitlow, Adam Sanchez, Juan Carlos Meza, and especially Mike Pleiss, by profession a chemist, who lends his time, talent, and smiling demeanor to us in the kitchen "just for the fun of it" every time we do a series.

More than anyone, I'm thankful to Jean-Claude Szurdak, who worked alongside me preparing the dishes to be photographed for the book and then supervised their preparation—along with the recipes on all the other shows—as the back kitchen manager for the series. I count on his innate knowledge of food and his good humor to make everything we do together great fun.

Producer's Acknowledgments

Producing *Jacques Pépin Fast Food My Way* with KQED has been a labor of love for me. I met Jacques in 1985 and formed a close relationship with him, his wife, Gloria, and his daughter, Claudine. In the 1970s, when I began working in the food industry, I was in awe of Jacques's extraordinary skills as a teacher, chef, and author. Even after working with him on 104 public television shows and three specials, I have never lost that sense of awe when watching him in the kitchen.

Of course, none of Jacques's series would have been possible without the sponsorship of companies devoted to quality. On this series, our thanks go to Cuisinart, maker of cookware and kitchen appliances, "Savor the Good Life"; www.mealtime.org, a resource for cooking with nutritious and convenient canned foods; and Oxo Good Grips, "tools you hold on to," for their support.

What a creative production team to collaborate with! Bruce Franchini is much more than a director. His involvement began in the conception of the show and continued throughout. His experience enriches all that we do. Associate producer Elizabeth Pepin (no relation to Jacques) and my assistant, Amy Vogler, made producing this show a pleasure from beginning to end. Their attention to every detail allowed me to do my best. Melinda Blau, an amazing volunteer, helped us all at every turn.

Our new set design was another collaborative achievement. Set designer TMG & Associates and set consultant Ron Haake translated our initial ideas, incorporated their own, and turned what we all hoped for into a reality. Scene 2 built our dream kitchen with all the quality of a home kitchen. Set stylist Tim Guetzlaff had an amazing eye for design and selected colors, materials, and props to create a comfortable kitchen for Jacques. Tehra Braren and the extraordinary staff at Sonoma Country Antiques provided the beautiful antique furniture on the set. Each day, prop and food stylist Claudia Sansone and assistant Lynne Mueller kept the set and dishes looking tiptop.

Our kitchen design was enhanced by the generous contributions of appliances by Sub-Zero/Wolf, stone counters by DuPont Zodiaq and Butler-Johnson, sinks and faucets by the Kohler Company, BHK Flooring by Golden State Flooring, rugs by Krimsa Fine Rugs and Décor, window coverings by Smith & Noble, beautiful artwork featuring lemons and apples by Silvia Gonzalez, and our favorite blue dog by Gary Steinborn of Venice Clay.

Thanks to the following companies for working with us to enhance the show with their wonderful products: Staub USA, Frank Maxwell and Associates, Vietri, Dover Metals Company, Riverside Design Group, Palecek, Trillium Design Imports, Salveson Korn Marketing, Domestique, Leonardo, Morgan & Company, the Bowl Mill, Peggy Karr Glass, Lamson & Goodnow, Aletha Soulé, Table de France, Venice Clay, Authentic Models, West Haven Designs, John Boos & Co., Chef'sChoice, Kuhn Rikon, Le Creuset, Rösle, Cuisipro, Pillivuyt France, Wüsthof-Trident of America, the Gardener, Brent Johnson, Houghton Mifflin Company, and the Levi's Brand.

Thank you to the entire staff of the back kitchen, particularly to Jean-Claude Szurdak and David Shalleck. Jean-Claude, Jacques's best friend, led the team through twenty-six shows in ten days. He is the kindest, most talented man one could imagine. David, our talented culinary producer, coordinated the food and equipment for the shows, providing Jacques with everything his recipes needed.

Beautiful ingredients and services were provided by Green-Leaf Produce, Clover Stornetta Farms, BiRite Foodservice Distributors, Osprey Seafood, Niman Ranch, Safeway stores, Whole Foods Market, Pacific Gourmet, Village Imports, Modesto Food Distributors, Straus Family Creamery, Scharffen Berger Chocolate Maker, Peet's Coffee & Tea, the Acme Bread Company, the Savannah Bee Company, Tazo Tea Company, Bella Cucina Artful Food, Byrd Cookie Company, the Glad Products Company, Vanilla, Saffron Imports, Allen & Cowley Specialty Foods, Anchor Brewing Company, College Inn Broth, Dundee Brandied Fruit Company, India Tree, Jelly Belly Candy Company, Olio Odessa Olive Oil, O Olive Oil, McEvoy Ranch, Red Hills Fruit Company, Marjorie Perotti-Brewster, David Rio Tea, Alsco American Linen Service, Oscartielle Equipment Company, and Maker's Mark.

A meal would be incomplete without wine. Thanks to Chambers & Chambers Wine Merchants, Rudd Vineyards & Winery, New Zealand Winegrowers, Champagne Mumm, and Champagne Perrier Jouët.

Thanks so much to the people at the Prescott Hotel, who made Jacques feel so at home.

All our hard work ends up in the hands of the editor. Paul Swenson has the thanks of everyone for his skillful editing of each show.

Above all, I thank Jacques. His professionalism, humor, knowledge, and love of life have made him one of the most revered chefs in the world today. We all feel so fortunate to have spent time with him, and I want to offer my sincere thanks to everyone, specifically mentioned or not, who helped create this memorable production.

—*Susie Heller*

Olives (*cont.*)

    Toasted Bread and Mozzarella, 39

Orange(s)

    and Cream Cheese, *174*, 206

    Sauce, 190, *191*

Oven-Baked Salmon with Sun-Dried Tomato and Salsa Mayonnaise, *118*, 118–19

Oysters, Smoked, Bean Puree with, 34

P

Parmesan

    for quick lavash pizza, 14

    Soupy Rice with Peas, 106

    Summertime Pasta, 110

Parsley

    and Pumpkin Seed Salad, 72

    for quick summer salad, 15

Pasta

    Bow-Tie, with Fried Eggs and Cheese, 62, *63*

    Ham, and Vegetable Gratin, *112*, 112–13

    Rigatoni and Mussels with Saffron, *140*, 140–41

    Summertime, 110

    Wonton Cannelloni in Tomato Sauce, 111

Pea(s)

    and Broccoli Rabe, 86, *87*

    frozen, buying, 99

    Instant Beef Tenderloin Stew, 156, *157*

    Pasta, Ham, and Vegetable Gratin, *112*, 112–13

    Puree of, with Mint and Cilantro, 99

    Soupy Rice with, 106

    Suprême of Chicken with Balsamic Vinegar and Shallot Sauce, 147, *147*

Peaches

    Caramelized, 208, *209*

    with Peach Sauce, 210, *211*

Pear(s)

    Brown Betty, 214

    in Honeyed Wine, 207

Pecan, Apple, and Apricot Crumble, 182, *183*

Pepper(s)

    Broiled Lamb Chops with Spinach, *154*, 169

    chile, adding to recipes, 42

    Green Hot Salsa, 42

    Grilled Striped Bass with Pimiento Relish, 117

    Oil, Halibut on Fresh Polenta with, *114*, 116

    Red Hot Salsa, 41

Pico de gallo, for quick dip, 12

Pimiento(s)

    Broiled Lamb Chops with Spinach, *154*, 169

    Relish, Grilled Striped Bass with, 117

Pineapple

    for quick cold drink, 17

    for quick dessert, 17

    Wedges in Caramel, *212*, 213

Pink Grapefruit Terrine, 190, *191*

Pinot Noir Granité, 199, *199*

Pizza, quick, preparing, 14

Plantains, Sautéed, 100

Poached Tilapia with Herbed Cream Sauce, 128

Polenta, Fresh, Halibut on, with Pepper Oil, *114*, 116

Pork

    Asparagus with Croutons and Chorizo, *82*, 84

    Chicken Bouillabaisse, 150–51, *151*

    Chops in Zesty Sauce, 164, *165*

    chorizo, for quick bean soup, 13

    cuts, for braising or stewing, 164

    cuts, for quick cooking, 164

    figs and prosciutto, for quick first course, 12

    ham cornucopias, for quick first course, 13

    Ham Steaks with Apricot-Mustard Glaze, 162

    Melon and Prosciutto, 43, *43*

    Pasta, Ham, and Vegetable Gratin, *112*, 112–13

    Red Snapper with Mussels and Chorizo, 124–26, *125*

    Sausage and Potato Packet, 168

    Scaloppine, Breaded, with Mushroom Sauce, 163

    Thirty-Minute Cassoulet, *166*, 167

Potato(es)

    Baked, with Chive Sour Cream, *105*, 108

    Beef Short Rib, and Mushroom Stew, 158

    Chicken Bouillabaisse, 150–51, *151*

    Codfish Brandade, 20–21

    Cubed, with Garlic and Sage, 109, *109*

    Instant Beef Tenderloin Stew, 156, *157*

    Red Snapper with Mussels and Chorizo, 124–26, *125*

    and Sausage Packet, 168

    sweet, chowder, quick, 14

Poultry. *See* Chicken; Quail

Praline Dessert, Vanilla, 217

Pressure-Cooker Lamb and White Bean Stew, *170*, 170–71

pressure cookers, about, 159